We Need to Talk

A MEMOIR ABOUT WEALTH

We Need to Talk

A MEMOIR ABOUT WEALTH

◆   ◆   ◆

Jennifer Risher

XENO

Library of Congress Cataloging-in-Publication Data

Names: Risher, Jennifer, 1965– author.
Title: We need to talk : a memoir about wealth / Jennifer Risher.
Description: First edition. | [Pasadena, CA] : Xeno, [2020]
Identifiers: LCCN 2019037244 (print) | LCCN 2019037245 (ebook) | ISBN 9781939096463 (casebound) | ISBN 9781939096647 (ebook)
Subjects: LCSH: Risher, Jennifer, 1965– | Millionaires—United States—Biography. | Wealth—United States.
Classification: LCC HC102.5.R536 R57 2020 (print) | LCC HC102.5.R536 (ebook) | DDC 305.5/234092 [B]—dc23
LC record available at https://lccn.loc.gov/2019037244
LC ebook record available at https://lccn.loc.gov/2019037245

The National Endowment for the Arts, the Los Angeles County Arts Commission, the Ahmanson Foundation, the Dwight Stuart Youth Fund, the Max Factor Family Foundation, the Pasadena Tournament of Roses Foundation, the Pasadena Arts & Culture Commission and the City of Pasadena Cultural Affairs Division, the City of Los Angeles Department of Cultural Affairs, the Audrey & Sydney Irmas Charitable Foundation, the Kinder Morgan Foundation, the Meta & George Rosenberg Foundation, the Allergan Foundation, the Riordan Foundation, Amazon Literary Partnership, and the Mara W. Breech Foundation partially support Red Hen Press.

First Edition
Published by Xeno Books
an imprint of Red Hen Press
www.redhen.org

Printed in Canada

for David and the girls

CONTENTS

INTRODUCTION

In 1991, at twenty-five years old, I took a job at Microsoft and got lucky. The guy behind me in line at orientation started up a conversation, telling me his name was David. He'd been an intern at Microsoft the previous summer and had accepted a position as a product manager. He made small talk and asked about me, his dark almond-shaped eyes practically closing as he smiled. I had no idea he was my future husband, but I smiled too.

Years later, when David and I were married and expecting our first child, we made a pivotal decision. David had been offered a job at a small, unknown startup selling books on the internet. As Bill Gates tried to keep him at Microsoft, where we both had stock options, I encouraged him to follow his heart. He loved books and technology. Three months later, David had joined that small startup, called Amazon.com, and I got lucky again. We both did. The company went public, and suddenly, in our early thirties, we had tens of millions of dollars.

For years, I'd told myself money didn't buy happiness, secretly believing it just might. I also thought I knew what it would be like to be rich, that a million dollars had the power to change everything. But our sudden new wealth didn't make my life perfect. I was still me. I hadn't escaped my worries, insecurities, or limitations, and was no more glamorous or confident. My childhood beliefs and habits remained, for better and worse.

Soon, I was discovering that my perception of the rich was inaccurate and incomplete. Wealth wasn't just glitz, glamor, and perfection, or arrogance, corruption, and greed. Images of people toting designer handbags and toy poodles aboard private jets and lounging on mega-yachts smoking cigars and guzzling champagne were extremely narrow depictions of affluence. The characters in *The Great Gatsby*, the men in *The Wolf of Wall Street*, and the women in *The Real Housewives* were ridiculously misleading examples of the rich as well.

The wealthy are more diverse and ordinary than most people see or believe. Eight out of ten of us grew up middle-class or poor, only one in ten inherited money, and most aren't living in Hollywood or working on Wall Street. We are hidden in plain sight, doing our grocery shopping, driving kids in carpool, and taking the subway to the office. We want to make a difference at our jobs and spend quality time with family and friends— and our numbers are growing. Even with the dot-com crash in 2001 and the housing crisis and recession of 2008, wealth at the top of the economic ladder has continued to explode. At the end of 2016, not counting primary residence, eleven million US households were worth $1 million, with over a million worth $5 million or more.

When I reached out to people whose circumstances were like my own and asked to interview them for this book, most told me they never discussed money but were interested in talking as long as they could remain anonymous.

In the pages that follow, you will meet Mary, who earns a high salary and has inherited wealth.

"I'll always work. I'll never have enough. I get a lot out of my job," she said. Then, after a few minutes, she added, "I'm not sure my self-esteem is up to not having a job. My identity depends on my position and success."

You will meet Laurie, who feels judged by her siblings because of the success of her husband's business.

"Maybe it's my issue, but I get stressed about birthday gifts," she said. "My sisters seem to expect something big. I never know what to do. Their expectations make me feel as though a nice new shirt isn't good enough."

You'll hear from Betsy, who worked in finance, taught her children the importance of staying within a budget, yet has been dismayed by how much they overspend, going out to eat and having food delivered.

"It's a problem. I'm not sure what to do," she said. "My husband and I try to set limits, but the limits are artificial—and our kids know it."

When her oldest moved back home for a month, and ended up staying for six, Betsy wasn't happy with the situation. She and her husband could afford to rent him an apartment but wanted him to learn to live within his own means.

"I've started charging him rent," Betsy said. "It's backfiring. He owes me money. But he knows the situation is contrived. What am I going to do? Kick him out?"

You'll meet Nicole, a corporate real estate developer who

has children in high school and college, but still pays for a full-time nanny.

"She's been with us for twenty-one years," Nicole said. "I don't need her anymore, but I can't bring myself to cut down her hours. She needs the job."

You'll meet others as well, but mostly you will get to know me. After growing up with middle-class values, saving my pennies, and being wary of the rich, I was embarrassed to join their ranks. My identity and place in the world were at stake. It took many years to get comfortable. Over the last decades, I've had a friend ask for $25,000, and another tell me she almost didn't invite our family to join hers to see a Cirque du Soleil show, concerned we'd only want seats they couldn't afford. I've worried about our children lacking motivation, discovered philanthropy isn't as straightforward as just writing a check, and grappled with the meaning of "enough"—not life or death issues, but real when living with them day to day.

Now in my fifties, I am profoundly grateful for the abundance in my life. Money has afforded me incredible freedom and allowed for extravagance and generosity. Our family has lived abroad and traveled the world, shared with relatives and friends, and donated amounts large and small. But there is a huge and growing problem in our country. It doesn't feel right that some people have more money than they can spend in a lifetime while nearly 40 million Americans are living in poverty. I should pay more taxes. Minimum wage should be higher. I'd like to see the government prioritize human well-being over financial gain and put a system in place that helps redistribute the wealth at the top to ensure food, education, healthcare, and housing for all.

I'm not an economist or a politician. I'm not some poor little rich girl either. Nor is my story a prescriptive account of how to do "rich" right. I don't have all the answers. I began writing because wealth surprised me. I wanted to reveal money for what it is and what it's not. I continued writing because everyone's voice adds to our country's conversation and hearing other people's stories helps us understand our own. In the end, I hope this book becomes a catalyst for conversation. Talking about money and how it makes us feel could help demystify wealth. We have a lot to learn from one another. More importantly, by talking, we could break down divides and confirm we are all ninety-nine percent the same.

Chapter One

THE TOSS

Two years out of college, unaware of the good fortune heading my way, I moved to Seattle with my best friend, Donna, and began looking for a job. I scoured the want ads and sent out resumes, serious about a career. My hope was to land an entry-level position in advertising. But I couldn't even get an interview. All the downtown agencies had long lines at the door.

After weeks of looking, I began to do temp work, handling customer complaint calls and alphabetizing files. Every evening, when I returned to my apartment, my fingers were crossed in anticipation. Maybe there'd be a message from a potential employer waiting for me on my answering machine. But the light on my phone was rarely blinking. The only calls I got were from my mother.

"How's the job search?" she asked.

"Okay," I lied.

"And the apartment?"

"It's fine. A bit empty. I saw a sofa I like, but I'm not going to buy it until I have a job."

"Sounds wise," she said with approval. "How's Donna doing?"

"She's fine. She's always busy," I said. "She loves her job."

Hanging up, I sat back in the wooden chair at my desk, alone. Best friends since high school, Donna and I had moved to Seattle together, but when she started her new job at a computer company, Donna had disappeared. We rarely saw one another.

Finally, after months of sending resumes and making follow-up calls, I got an informational interview at a small agency downtown. Hoping for my big break, I arrived early and walked around the block several times before entering the building. After only a few minutes in the lobby, I saw a man in a flannel shirt and corduroy pants sauntering toward me, looking as though he'd just dropped by the office to water his favorite plant. I couldn't have conjured up someone more approachable. He introduced himself as Dave and gave me a tour of the agency, nodding as I pitched myself as a hard worker, eager to learn.

"I'm afraid we just don't have any openings," he said. "But let me introduce you to our HR guy, Jan. Maybe he knows something I don't."

Dave took me downstairs, stopping outside an office where a woman in her early twenties was slapping high fives with a man wearing a silky black tie covered in bubblegum machines.

"So, you want to work in advertising," Jan said after Dave introduced us.

"I have a resume with me," I said. "Would you like to see it?"

"Sure, why not?"

Bobbing his head at my resume, Jan asked about my summer work experience, then told me there were only three entry-level account coordinator positions at the agency. All of them were taken.

"I just don't have anything," he said.

"Could you use extra help? I'll work for free."

My mouth made the proclamation before my head had the chance to approve the material. But I wasn't sorry. Working in advertising had been a dream of mine for years. I was finally inside an agency and wanted to stay.

Jan didn't seem the type often at a loss for words, but he froze for a moment.

"Okay," he finally said. "I like the attitude. The Nordstrom team could use your help. We'll see you Monday morning."

The next week, I began showing up early and doing whatever was needed, excited to experience the inner workings of advertising. I also started to make work friends. And after more than a month of helping full-time, when one of my new friends told me about an opening at McCann Erickson, the big agency across the street, I rushed my resume over and landed the job. Finally! I had a paid position. My goal had been accomplished. My career was underway.

My days at McCann Erickson were spent running between the account management and creative departments, shepherding projects through production. I did a lot of grunt work too, making photocopies and serving coffee to clients. I came in early, left late, and worked on the weekends, keeping the job files up to date and making sure everything was in order. Meanwhile, earning $19,500 a year, it was tough to get through the month with enough left to pay rent. I rarely went out, cut coupons, rode the bus, brought my lunch to the office, and rationed my coffee. At a time when Seattle's very own Starbucks was becoming a national phenomenon, I only allowed myself a $1.65 drink once a week. It felt important to watch every dollar. Managing my money made me feel responsible.

One day, after nearly a year at the agency, as I sat on the floor, sorting photocopies in a skirt and heels, dressed for the job I hoped to earn, not the one I had, I got an important phone call. Seemingly out of the blue, this call was a peace offering of sorts. Two years earlier, before arriving in Seattle, Donna and I had planned a move to San Francisco. We'd talked about sharing an apartment and looking for jobs together. Then, a week before our move, Donna broke the news that she'd accepted a position at a computer company in Seattle. Initially, I'd been crushed but ended up moving to Seattle with her.

"Hi. It's me," Donna said. "Do you have a minute?"

"Sure," I told her. "But I can't talk long."

A rule follower, I felt uncomfortable taking personal calls during work hours.

"There's an opening here in campus recruiting," Donna said. "I know you don't want to work in HR, but I thought you should know about the job. Are you interested?"

Unaware of the gold coin floating into the air, I took a few moments to think. The photocopying was getting old, but I didn't want to leave advertising. There was so much still to be learned about targeting customers and positioning products. An HR job hiring business school graduates into marketing positions didn't sound that appealing. But I missed Donna's friendship and imagined we'd be more connected if we worked at the same company. I was also intrigued by Microsoft, the company where she worked. After nearly two years in Seattle, I knew Microsoft represented challenge and opportunity.

There were great perks too: free soft drinks, cafeterias with latte stands, and a membership to the health club right down the street. Maybe if I got in the door, I could wrangle myself a marketing job from the inside. With that thought, I told Donna I was interested in an interview—and the gold coin landed. One moment, one answer, and the trajectory of my life was about to change.

Unlike the sleek, image-conscious world of advertising where we dressed to impress clients, Microsoft was full of boys in T-shirts practically living in their offices, spending days and nights writing code. It was 1991. While the rest of the country was recovering from a minor recession, Microsoft was booming. The workforce had outgrown its original pod of six white '80s-style structures, and several new brick buildings were under construction. The halls buzzed with energy, and inside each office, employees stared intently into computer screens or scribbled furiously on whiteboards, on a mission to put a computer on every desktop. Windows 3.0, the newest version of the company's operating system, had launched a year earlier to huge success, and with the average age of thirty, employees were out to change the world. It was an exciting time to be at the company.

After several long, demanding interviews, I got a call with an offer, and accepted immediately, excited about becoming part of the action. My starting salary was $26,000, a big step up from what I'd been making, and I barely listened as my new manager, Jane, explained the biannual reviews, bonuses, salary increases, and stock options.

At the time, employee stock options were a complete unknown. Even within Microsoft, no one truly understood what options were or how they worked. No other company had ever granted so many options to so many employees, and without history as a reference, it was impossible to know what to expect. Certainly, no one at Microsoft was talking about their compensation. Everyone prided themselves on being nothing like the brokers and bankers of Wall Street who were making money with money and bragging about their bonuses. Intelligence, hard work, and a passion for technology were currency at Microsoft. While it was clear that options were a benefit, they were viewed as a bunch of numbers on paper, completely unrelated to everyday life.

But in time, options began making us rich.

Midway through my second year at Microsoft, as a quarter of my options vested, I took a closer look—and was astonished. The Microsoft stock price had been moving steadily upwards since my first day, and after eighteen months at the company, I had tens of thousands of dollars of free money in my future. I couldn't believe it. If the stock price continued to climb, in another three years, my options would be worth as much as $300,000. Three hundred thousand dollars!

Four years earlier, after graduating from college and before moving to Seattle, I'd worked at a steel company in Tokyo teaching English to executives. I thought of my time in Japan as a final hurrah, a chance to follow my heart and have one last adventure before settling down and starting a career. I'd known nothing about Japan, and loved my time in Tokyo. Living in company housing and benefitting from the power of the yen, I unexpectedly returned home feeling rich, not only from the experience, but from the money I'd saved.

"I can buy a new car," I'd bragged to my father.

"You *think* you have a lot," he'd cautioned. "You need to be careful with your money."

As usual, my dad had been right. Twenty-four thousand dollars had sounded like a fortune, but after buying a car and working for free, I'd depleted my savings. But Microsoft stock options were different. My fortune was so much bigger. In fact, $300,000 was an uncomfortably large sum. I never considered telling my parents. If they knew, I was worried they'd look at me differently. I didn't want my options to create a distance between us, my place in our family at risk. Where would I fit in if I had more money than my father? My mother wouldn't approve of me having so much either. She wasn't comfortable with wealth or the wealthy.

◆　◆　◆

July 15, 1991, my first day at Microsoft, Donna introduced me to Lynn, another campus recruiter who fast became a friend. Lynn's sharp wit and strong opinions made her fun to be around. Many mornings, the two of us walked to the cafeteria together, Lynn giving me the scoop on the heroes and villains within each department and offering advice on how to create effective interview questions. We laughed about Bill Clinton's failure to inhale and scrutinized the relationship she was beginning with a man named Adam, a program manager at Microsoft.

At the end of August, campus recruiters were required to

attend farewell parties for the interns who'd been working at the company for the summer. Lynn and Donna had gone to these events in the past and weren't excited. But I couldn't wait. The parties were being held at the home of Bill Gates. Not only was Bill highly respected throughout the company, he was practically a billionaire. Going to his house meant seeing how he lived.

On the evening of the first party, I drove into the upper-class neighborhood of Laurelhurst and searched for the address, which was right on Lake Washington. Spotting the house, I pulled forward, parked, and felt disappointed. The dark green Craftsman looked like any other large home. It didn't scream rich or have a special aura of sophistication. There was no Bentley in the driveway, no butler at the door. I walked up the front path, was directed down the stairs, and my disappointment grew. The rooms were not grand. Gorgeous artwork did not grace the walls. There were no fine pieces of furniture or elegant antiques. Nothing about Bill's home was flashy or glamorous. With its worn leather sofas, wood-paneled walls, and pool table, the basement, from which we gained access to the backyard where dinner was served, looked like a bachelor pad stuck in the 1970s.

After a perfectly nice evening talking with interns and their managers, while the view of the water was beautiful and the food delicious, I remained baffled. I'd hoped to see inside the life of the rich, and nothing about the evening came close to fulfilling my expectations. I didn't understand why Bill wasn't living in one of those spectacular mansions I'd seen in movies and on TV. I thought the wealthy lived stylish lives in rambling manors and enjoyed showing off their success. What was Bill doing with all his money?

In the fall, our team of twelve campus recruiters traveled the country, giving presentations at top colleges and universities. In the winter, we conducted interviews at Microsoft in Redmond, looking for people who were smart, hardworking, and could get things done. As each candidate talked with employees doing the jobs they would do if hired, campus recruiters read feedback over email and made sure the best and the brightest met with key decision makers. Those failing to reach the bar returned to our offices to wrap up the day. No one at Microsoft wanted to waste precious time with someone who wasn't a good fit for the company.

Lynn and Donna handled the recruiting process for college undergraduates applying for test and development positions, while I worked with the MBA candidates interested in product management and marketing. In the early 1990s, most business school graduates were out to land high-paying jobs in corporate banking, consumer products companies, and consulting firms like Goldman Sachs, Procter & Gamble, and Deloitte & Touche. Since Microsoft was relatively unknown—way out in the boonies of Washington State—and offered salaries below industry standard and the unfamiliar benefit of employee stock options, the MBAs who interviewed were entrepreneurial in spirit, not necessarily looking to get rich.

In the spring, making offers over the phone, I did my best to explain how stock options worked: the strike price of an option was set the first week on the job and each option was worth the difference between that strike price and the stock's current market value. After eighteen months at the company, a quarter of an employee's stock option grant was vested, which meant it was available for cash. Every six months after that, another eighth of the grant vested and the full amount could be cashed-in after four-and-a-half years.

"If you work hard, you'll help drive the stock price up," I said. "If the price goes up $50 in the next four-and-a-half years, your grant of 2,000 options will be worth $100,000. If the stock goes up $100, you'll have twice as much."

Even though I understood stock options in theory, I'd had no idea what they really meant until I'd been at Microsoft for eighteen months and my own options began vesting. Then, seeing a potential $300,000 in my future, I ran into the office next door and took my usual seat in the chair opposite my co-worker, Stephen.

Stephen and I had started the same day, were doing the same job, and spent many hours together, discussing candidates and interview strategies. We'd shared company gossip, savored juicy anecdotes about our love interests, discussed religion, and argued politics. Although we'd never talked about money, it seemed reasonable to slap a private high five in acknowledgment of our mutual good fortune.

"Do you realize what we have?" I asked. "Our options are worth $300,000."

Stephen stared at me in silence.

"I'm not comfortable talking about this," he murmured, glancing at the open door. He then lowered his voice and confided, "You know, I accepted my job offer earlier than you did, right before a stock split. I have more. You can't say anything, but I have over a half-million dollars."

It was my turn to stare. We had started the same day. We were doing the same job. I couldn't believe Stephen had twice as much as I did.

I leaned back in my chair and looked out the window at the construction across the street. Attempting to appear casual, I asked Stephen about his girlfriend. We talked about the positions we both needed to fill. And as soon as enough time had elapsed, I excused myself and headed down the hall.

"Can two people who started the same day, who are doing the same job have vastly different stock option grants?" I asked Jane, our manager, as I burst into her office.

Jane turned from her desk.

"Are you thinking about a specific case?"

"I know it's not something I should be talking about, but does Stephen really have twice as many stock options as I do?"

The words hung in the air. Blood rushed to my face. What was I doing? It wasn't any of my business. I shouldn't be talking about Stephen behind his back. I shouldn't be so interested in money either. The Microsoft culture scorned a focus on personal financial reward. It was cool to be smart, technical, and strategic, to be creating cutting-edge software and outpacing the competition. Talking about money was evidence of misplaced values and greed. I wasn't being the responsible woman my mother had raised.

At ten years old, when I asked how much my father made, my mother frowned and turned away. His salary was none of my business. On those special occasions, when our family went out for dinner, my mother scolded me for peering at the check at the end of the meal. It was improper and unladylike to care about cost. I needed to avert my eyes and let my father handle the finances.

"I shouldn't be talking about this," I mumbled to Jane.

"You're right. It's not up for discussion," Jane said.

But my concern wasn't about money alone. Stephen and I were doing the same work. Our goals were identical. We were both good employees. Where was the justice in him having so much more?

"Aren't Stephen and I both doing a good job?" I asked.

"Yes," Jane said. "But he accepted his offer in May, before he graduated. With the three-for-two stock split in June, he had more when he started. Your offer came after that split."

"That's not fair!" I exclaimed. "Our start date was the same."

"That's true."

"Isn't there something you can do?"

"Look, we're all lucky. Just appreciate what you have. Stop looking around at other people."

"I'm not. It's just . . ."

"It's just the way things are," Jane said, turning in her chair and ending the conversation.

Back in the safety of my office, I closed the door and sat down. Gazing at my computer screen, frustrated and upset by the inequity, I moved the cursor in small angry circles. Then, letting out my breath, I slumped back in my chair. I wanted to crawl under my desk. I couldn't believe I'd just stormed into my boss's office and betrayed a friend's trust.

From within the small world of recruiting at Microsoft, surrounded by friends and co-workers who were benefitting from employee stock options, and without much experience in the workforce, I lacked perspective on money and life. Looking back, I still see the unfairness of Stephen's compensation being higher than mine, but there was unfairness in everything happening with stock options at Microsoft in the 1990s. A bunch of employees in their late twenties and early thirties were becoming wildly rich. We may have made some smart decisions along the way and were helping put a computer on every desktop, working eighty-hour weeks but the amount of money we were gaining was way out of proportion to anything any of us were doing or had done. As a twenty-something kid, wrapped up in the moment and in myself, I didn't yet understand my own crazy good luck, let alone comprehend the reality of having so much money.

◆ ◆ ◆

Though it was upsetting that Stephen had more money than I did, in a matter of weeks, stock options faded back into the future where they'd been hiding for the previous eighteen months, more an abstraction than part of everyday life. For Stephen and me, it was work as usual. We never spoke of our options again.

Two years after starting at Microsoft, I began contemplating a move from recruiting to marketing, and when a product manager from the Consumer Division contacted campus recruiting in search of an entry-level marketer to help launch a new software product code-named *Utopia*, I walked my resume to his office and told him I wanted the job.

"If you join a product group, you'll be at the bottom of the pay scale," Donna warned. "You won't get an increase. I doubt you'll get more stock."

I appreciated Donna's counsel but didn't care about a raise or additional options. I was hoping to learn more about marketing and contribute directly to Microsoft's bottom line. *Utopia* was intriguing too. It was such a creative product, offering an intuitive way to work on a home computer. In fact, *Utopia*'s revolutionary social interface was attracting attention within the company. There was even talk of Melinda French heading up the project.

Melinda had gone on a recruiting trip with me to UCLA the previous fall and was already my idol. Smart and straightforward, she was one of the best interviewers at the company and a big-deal manager. Even at the time, it wouldn't have been a stretch to imagine the impact she would have on philanthropy, focusing on improving the lives of underserved women and girls across the globe. But as I thought about working for Melinda and considered the notoriously tough questions that were asked during the interview process, I got nervous. Was I up for the challenge? Was I smart enough for the job? How would I answer all those questions? Why were manhole covers round? What animal did I want to be? How would I market a car to someone in a wheelchair? How could I get my grandmother to buy Excel? I didn't know much about marketing and was worried about not having good ideas or the right thing to say. Then, I thought of David.

On my first day, at orientation, he had been standing behind me in line, wearing shockingly bright blue shorts. He told me about being an intern the previous summer, and about the job he was starting as a product manager for the company's first database. Later, by email, a mode of communication unknown to me and most of the world but ubiquitous at Microsoft, David had asked me out.

It sounded like a bad idea to date someone at work, but the company was big, he was cute, and soon we were spending a couple of hours together in the dark, watching *Terminator 2: Judgment Day*. Over dinner afterward, David told me his favorite joke about a duck. He also laughed at my favorite about an orange and a banana, and grinned when I mentioned my favorite quote from Joseph Conrad's *Heart of Darkness*.

"You mean, 'I don't like work—no man does, but I like what is in the work, the chance to find yourself'?" he said.

"That's the one!"

"That was the quote I put in my college yearbook," he told me.

Believing, as Conrad suggested, that work helped me connect with myself, I'd copied that same quote into my journal during college. Whenever truly engrossed in an activity, I felt self-consciousness fall away and time disappear, allowing me to get in touch with an essential part of my being. Did David see and understand that? Was he someone with whom I could truly connect?

For our second date, he invited me to dinner at his apartment. Answering the door wearing an apron and holding a knife, he swept his arm wide to usher me into his living room. Two brown plaid loveseats sat opposite one another, and piles of books and unpacked cardboard boxes were spread across the floor. An old TV was perched in one corner, its rabbit-ear antennae leaning against the window as though seeking fresh air. Several intriguing items sat proudly on an otherwise empty bookshelf: a tiny blue-wire bicycle, a yellow rubber duck in a sailor's hat, a green plastic crocodile, and a glass bottle of blue ink. I wanted to walk over to get a closer look at these treasures, in search of additional information about the man who had invited me to dinner, but propriety compelled me to follow David to the kitchen.

"How can I help?" I asked.

He leaned over a cookbook and frowned down at a recipe, assuring me everything was under control. The mess of wooden spoons and mixing bowls didn't seem to bother him. He reached for a spice jar and plastic measuring spoons. Then, crouching slightly, holding a teaspoon, he extracted just the right amount of thyme, which he sprinkled carefully into a small glass bowl.

"To taste," he read aloud, his finger on the recipe. "How do you measure that?"

His goofy humor was endearing. So was his methodical approach. Watching him attempt to wrap a flattened pork loin around a filling of prunes and apricots, pushing at the dried fruit with his fingers and fumbling with a piece of string clearly dug up from somewhere far from the kitchen and cut way too short, I wanted to give him a hug. He was so earnest. So sweet.

Over dinner, we talked about our experiences at college. Both of us had graduated in 1987 with liberal arts degrees, me with a BA from Connecticut College where I'd majored in art history and minored in philosophy, David with a degree from

Princeton University where he studied French and comparative literature. He seemed impressed by the two years I'd worked in Tokyo. I found him impressive too. After Princeton, he'd worked in consulting for two years, spent three months biking across the country with a friend, and had then gone to Harvard Business School. But he hadn't gotten an MBA as a matter of course. He'd applied to Harvard on a whim and, when he got in, decided to go.

In the months that followed, David and I met after work for late dinners and watched a lot of movies. As we took long walks around our neighborhood, we discovered we shared a similarly open, liberal perspective on life and the world. Many weekends, we got together with Donna and Lynn from recruiting and their boyfriends, Matt and Adam, the six of us talking non-stop about Microsoft.

But while we got along well and had fun together, when I tried to get close, David pulled away. I'd suggest spending a night at the coast and he claimed to need "alone time." He didn't want to hang out all weekend either. He needed space. Although it was becoming painfully clear he didn't want the same intimacy I craved, I couldn't walk away. He was so smart, so funny, so easy to be around. He gave me a sense of belonging. I felt understood. Then, one evening, when I answered the phone in his apartment, his former girlfriend was on the other end of the line. I handed him the receiver and walked out the door in tears.

It turned out David had moved from Boston to Seattle without completely letting go of a four-year relationship. When he revealed his old girlfriend was going to visit for a weekend, I told him I didn't want to see him anymore. It was too difficult to know he cared for someone else.

But our breakup had been months in the past and, eager to get help preparing for interviews, I steeled myself and gave him a call. Right away, he agreed to meet and suggested Victrola, a coffee shop the two of us had frequented as a couple. Walking in the door, and seeing him at our table, wearing one of his many striped T-shirts, I wanted to run over and jump into his lap. Instead, I waved and strolled to the counter where I ordered a nonfat latte. I then pulled up a chair opposite my old boyfriend and thanked him in advance for sharing his knowledge about marketing.

The following week, I had my first interview with Karen, the visionary behind *Utopia*. Afterward, I met with Melinda, who had just taken the position as group product manager. Quickly putting me at ease, Melinda sat casually on a table in front of a white board. Rather than peppering me with questions, as I'd anticipated, she posed hypothetical marketing problems that we contemplated together. We debated how to position a product and considered the best way to reach customers. The discussion was fun. When the conversation ended, I skipped back to my office.

The next day, I was skipping again—right across campus and into the building where David worked.

"I got the job!" I shouted.

Bringing my arms down around David's neck, I forgot we weren't a couple. With a kiss, we were together again. Well, almost. He told me he'd been confused, that his old girlfriend had been going through a hard time, but that her visit to Seattle had been the end of their relationship. He then told me he'd been thinking about me, surprised at how much he missed me. I too was surprised. I'd never broken up and gotten back together with anyone before and didn't want to be *that* person who wasn't clear about her feelings. But I wanted to be with David. The two of us were in sync. We found the same things funny and shared a similar view of life. We complemented one another too, me helping him get in touch with his emotions and him helping me find words for my feelings.

For our official second-time-around first date, David and I spent an afternoon at Green Lake, the best place in Seattle to enjoy a sunny afternoon. At first, as we walked the perimeter of the lake, I felt myself talking way too much. When we sat down together on the grass and watched people walking by, he couldn't sit still. He jumped up and pulled me up with him.

"Let's rent a paddle boat," he said, heading to the dock.

Sitting side by side, cruising through the lily pads past the ducks, we raced from the shore, challenging one another to see who could pedal faster and who would tire first. Finally, we let the boat drift. I leaned back and closed my eyes, happy to be next to David.

"Hey, stop!" I said as sprinkles of water hit my face. "Who knows what's in that lake water?"

David smiled. He stood up, pulled his shirt over his head, and let his pants drop. Wearing nothing but boxers, as if to prove he wouldn't splash anything on me that he wouldn't mind being submerged in himself, he dove into the water.

"Feels great. Want to join me?" he asked, popping up seconds later, his skin shining green through the murk. "I love you," he added.

His words took me by surprise, filling me with joy and opening me up to how much I cared about him too. I'd missed his smarts and goofiness. Could he be my forever partner? I smiled, imagining a future together.

"I love you too," I said.

Contemplation & Conversation

- Was it good luck or good decisions that helped Jennifer land the Microsoft job? Do you attribute your successes and failures to circumstances, luck, choices, or talent?

- Jennifer had preconceived ideas about the way the rich live. What do you believe about people who have a lot of money?

- Was Jennifer wrong to talk to her boss about her stock options? Do you talk about money or your salary with co-workers?

Chapter Two

STUCK IN THE PAST

The summer before I started seventh grade, our family moved to a small town in rural Oregon where my father purchased twenty acres and planted a vineyard, dreaming of eventually retiring to work the land. He then continued working as a corporate insurance broker, commuting an hour each way to and from Portland while my mother, who had stayed home for twelve years with my younger brother and me, took a position as the librarian for the local public schools.

Two years after our move, during my freshman year in high school, I met Donna. She had a gregarious personality and was always surrounded by friends. She was a good listener too. When no one else got it, Donna understood. We shared a love for baking and an obsession for fashion. We were also accomplices in toilet paper raids and competitors on the public high school tennis courts. Donna was drawn to my family as well, captivated by my mother's love of books and intrigued by my father. Most dads in Dayton, Oregon were farmers, truck drivers, or cabinet makers, and she thought it was cool mine wore a suit and drove to the city every weekday.

One day, while listening to Rod Stewart and munching

on homemade chocolate chip cookies out of the freezer in our kitchen, Donna and I had one of our many serious talks about life.

"What would you do if you had a million dollars?" she asked me.

"Have a cute boyfriend," I said.

"Yeah. Me too."

We didn't consider who these guys were. We weren't concerned where they came from. Did we plan to buy them? We seemed to believe a million dollars would make us more attractive. Perhaps the guys were only after our money. We didn't care. A million dollars was going to flip a switch, create magic, fulfill our dreams, and make life perfect. I imagined myself more relaxed and a lot more carefree. After all, didn't money have the power to change everything?

"I'd buy a dark green Porsche," I told Donna.

"No, really," she pressed. "If you had a million dollars, what would you *really* do? Buy something for your parents? Have a big party? Would you still go to school?"

At sixteen, I just wanted the guy and the car.

While I was growing up, there had always been a rainy day lurking in the living room. My mother stuck closely to her grocery list, used the same teabag for a second and third cup of tea, and only drove when necessary because gas was expensive. When my father sat at his desk, opening envelopes and paying bills in clouds of cigarette smoke, I tiptoed past. Finances made him grumpy.

The oldest of five, my father had grown up in Middletown,

New York where he rushed to the dinner table to gulp down his food before someone else could claim it. His father had dropped out of school in eighth grade to work and his mother was a second-grade teacher. The family didn't have much money. Although my grandfather worked his way up in a bank, eventually becoming branch president, my father continued to worry about getting enough to eat. Meanwhile, my mother, an only child, grew up upper middle-class in Flint, Michigan. Her father was a prominent lawyer, her mother a volunteer on the local hospital board, and both were keenly aware of proper etiquette. They participated in a theater group and bridge club and were careful to keep up appearances. When she was scrubbing the floor in a housecoat and curlers and a stranger rang the doorbell, my grandmother put on an accent and pretended to be the help.

"The lady of the house isn't home," she said.

My parents met as students at Brown University. My father graduated first, and while my mother finished college and earned a master's of library science at Columbia University, he traveled the country, working at a hotel in Miami, then earning money by driving a pink Cadillac from Las Vegas to New York before taking a more permanent position at an insurance company. After my parents got married, they moved to Seattle to escape the cold East Coast winters, my father taking another insurance job and my mother becoming a librarian at the Seattle Public Library.

Although their backgrounds were different, like most in their generation, my parents considered themselves solidly middle-class and were careful with money. For the first year of their marriage, they rented a basement apartment, saving for a down payment on a house of their own, finally purchasing a single-story home in a family-friendly neighborhood full of small, eager houses. In 1965, when I was born, my mother stopped working. My brother, Michael, arrived two years later, and for more than a decade, my mother did her best to be a good mother and housewife. When my father returned home after a long day at the office, she greeted him with a kiss. She also made dinner, ironed his blue and white button-down shirts, and taught my brother and me the importance of reading, not spending much money, and home-cooked meals shared as a family every night at seven o'clock.

Meanwhile, my father, the breadwinner, was head of the household, in charge of finances. He also spent hours in the yard on weekends, planting shrubs and digging in the dirt. When I was five, he gave me my first job, telling me he'd pay me to pick up magnolia leaves from the front walkway. With my mother watching and my brother helping, I filled two grocery bags with leaves and waited all afternoon for my father to come home.

"Is that all?" he joked, pulling the bags over to his big leather chair. "Two, four, six . . . ten, twelve, fourteen, sixteen . . ."

His counting sounded strange, but he knew what he was doing. My dad knew everything. Paying me a penny for every two leaves I'd picked up, he placed coins in my hand.

"It isn't much," he warned. "You'll want to keep your money safe."

Feeling my father's attention and love infused in each cent, I put the coins in my piggybank, which I hid in my room.

Then, when I could write my first and last name by heart, my mother whisked me to the bank, proud of my new skill and excited that I could start saving like a grown-up. I signed the application, deposited my cash, and watched as my mother contributed fifty dollars of her own. She then told her parents about my new account.

"I'm going to buy fifty dollars' worth of Montana Power and Light in your name," my grandfather told me. "We'll see which fifty earns more over time: the money in the bank or the money in the stock market."

Surrounded by adults who equated saving with being good, I never considered spending my money. The only acceptable time to let go of cash was during the holidays. Even then, although crass to mention, price was a consideration. For days, my mother deliberated over what to get my grandparents, weighing the benefits of an electric carving knife against those of a crockpot and talking about each with my father over dinner.

Glitter, felt, and glue were part of our Christmas routine too, my mother assuring Michael and me that what we created at home for our aunts and uncles was much more meaningful than anything we could buy in a store. We also kept a small pine in a pot outside, and at the beginning of December, my father wheeled the tree into the house and Michael and I decorated it with homemade strands of cranberries and popcorn, and ornaments dug out of the Christmas box retrieved from the attic. On Christmas morning, we woke early to open the gifts in our stockings from Santa, then gawked at all the presents under the tree.

When I was six, my father got a promotion, and we left

our middle-class street in Seattle for a home set back from the road in a suburb of Portland. Michael and I had never been in such a huge house and were thrilled to have a floor to ourselves with a bathroom of our own. There was a large yard in the back with a stream and a tree house. But my mother didn't like our new upper-class neighborhood. Unbeknownst to me at the time, she viewed the neighbors as excessive with their fancy cars and lavish parties. Luckily for her, we didn't stay long. My father soon got another promotion and a transfer to London where we lived for two years, my mother much happier with the formality of the country and the fact that, as a foreigner, she was exempt from social norms.

When our family returned to the United States, my father was offered a senior position at his company's Los Angeles headquarters. But, uninterested in ratcheting up into what they believed would be an uncomfortably competitive, difficult-to-afford lifestyle, my parents decided my father should turn the offer down. Instead, we moved to rural Oregon where my father purchased twenty acres, planted a vineyard, and continued to work in insurance. My mother took a job as a librarian, Michael slipped seamlessly into fifth grade, and I started junior high and became friends with Donna.

◆　◆　◆

Twelve years after dreaming a million dollars could bring me a boyfriend and a car, I had David in my life and a lot of money in stock options. But when David suggested we spend the weekend together in San Francisco, I discovered my childhood habits and beliefs had a very strong hold on my thinking. At first, I was thrilled. It sounded fun to spend two days with my boyfriend, strolling through neighborhoods, visiting museums, and trying new restaurants. But when I called about flights and learned the airfare from Seattle to San Francisco was over $200, I didn't think we could go. Two hundred dollars was way too much to spend on only two nights away. But, not ready to give up on the trip entirely, I made some phone calls, checking with different airlines, searching for cheaper flights. And when I discovered we could fly to Oakland for $50 less than it cost to fly to San Francisco, I purchased tickets, excited about the savings.

For weeks, David and I looked forward to our getaway, but on the morning of our departure, we were stressed. The flight to Oakland left much earlier in the day than either of us would have chosen, and we had a lot of work to get done. I went into the office early and spent a couple of hours at my desk before rushing to David's building where he was waiting in the car, looking tense. Neither of us spoke as we sped to the airport and sprinted for the plane.

By the time we landed, we were talking again, but we couldn't just leave the airport and enjoy the afternoon. We had a distance to go. First, we had to take the shuttle to the BART station for the train to San Francisco. After finding the shuttle stop, we waited fifteen minutes for the bus to finally lumber around the corner, then spend ten minutes idling while the driver took a break. Once underway, we slowly wound our way through the city. Disembarking at the BART station, as other passengers hurried down the stairs to the train, we looked for where to buy tickets. Standing in front of the ticket machine, frantically flattening out dollar bills, we heard the train pulling away below. Then, with tickets in hand, after leaving work early, flying two hours, taking a shuttle to BART, we were still in a city that wasn't our destination, waiting for the train. I looked over at David. He looked at me. For a moment, we stared. Then we burst out laughing.

"What are we doing?" I asked. "This isn't what I imagined for our weekend away."

"Isn't getting there half the fun?"

"Maybe. But we could make some changes."

"Like fly directly to San Francisco at a more convenient time?" David suggested.

Our trip could have been a lot easier and more relaxed. We had so much money. Why did I care so much about saving fifty bucks? Not only did I have hundreds of thousands of dollars, David's options were worth an extraordinary amount. He'd joined Microsoft at a higher level, accepted his offer months before me, and like Stephen, benefited from a stock split. If the stock price remained strong, in the next few years, his options would be worth nearly two million dollars. Two million dollars! Shouldn't we be cracking open champagne? Where were the yachts, fancy cars, and first-class travel? We were rich! Wasn't all our money supposed to change everything? I didn't need to be so concerned about saving fifty dollars—but I was.

Eight months after spending the weekend in San Francisco, determined to take better advantage of our good fortune and have more fun, I suggested David and I spend three weeks together in Greece. At first, he couldn't imagine being away from Microsoft so long. He was fully entrenched in preparations for the launch of Access, Microsoft's first desktop database. But as I assured him the challenges weren't going away, and that vacations were good for the soul *and* productivity, he finally acquiesced.

Tickets to Europe were expensive, but with three weeks to delve into the culture and history, I could justify the expense. My family had always placed a high importance on travel and education. But when David proposed going business class, I recoiled. I didn't want to be one of *those people*, aloof and superior, looking down at everyone else as they trekked to the back. I'd long wondered who they were, imaging them leading extravagant lives. I'd read *The Great Gatsby* and knew about *Scrooge*, and didn't want to be anything like *those people*. Their place in the world was so different from mine.

But the real shock of business class was the price. Economy tickets from Seattle to Athens were already expensive at $700, and business-class seats were an eye-popping $2,000—each. It was reasonable to make changes but spending three times more than necessary just to get to our vacation didn't feel right. Besides, what would my mother think?

David was also surprised by the high cost of business class but didn't have the same fixation on saving or fear of excess. He wanted to experience twenty percent more legroom. Perhaps he was feeling his importance as a Microsoft product manager. More likely, his inner kid wanted to play, excited about free drinks and being closer to the pilot.

"Let's buy coach and upgrade with miles," he suggested.

Once again, I was unsure. I'd saved my miles for years,

happy to have them, just in case, for the future. It didn't make sense to use a whole 20,000 miles just to sit up front. How good could business class be? But with David assuring me using miles to upgrade extracted the most value possible out of each one, reminding me of my desire to take advantage of our good fortune and have more fun, it was my turn to acquiesce— but I didn't tell my parents. I kept the indulgence a secret from everyone we knew.

Boarding the plane to Athens, I was happy we didn't have to search for 36B or scramble for space in the overhead bins. Instead, a flight attendant greeted us by name. She whisked our coats away and returned seconds later to offer water, juice, and— champagne! We were then served a three-course meal on white china, after which, stretched out, completely reclined, with comforters and pillows, we actually slept. Business class was a lot more comfortable than sitting upright, squeezed between strangers. It was hard not to feel special, even a bit smug. Then we landed.

We took a taxi to the hotel I'd booked weeks in advance from Seattle. After checking in and hauling our bags through the dimly lit lobby, past the broken elevator, and up three flights of stairs, I looked over at David and started to laugh. My childhood was present once again.

When my family had lived in London, we'd taken weekend road trips to Stonehenge and Cornwall and stayed in reasonably-priced bed-and-breakfasts. Not only were B&Bs less expensive than hotels, we got to meet the locals and learn about the culture. We got to experience an authentic English breakfast too, complete with sausages, fried eggs, baked beans, mushrooms, cooked tomatoes, and toast. There was always more food than the four of us wanted or could eat, and we often ended up laughing at my mother as she hid sausages and toast in her purse, not wanting to appear rude or wasteful. Now, in Athens, maintaining the status quo, I was ensuring we had an authentic, local experience. I was proving my worth as responsible too, proud of being in sync with my childhood—and with the Microsoft company culture.

At the 1993 Microsoft company meeting, instead of celebrating our huge and growing success, employees were told to cut back, to forgo shrimp in favor of the cocktail wiener. Hearing the shrimp and weenies message delivered by Dana Carvey from *Saturday Night Live*—and not considering the expense of having the Church Lady as our host—we laughed. We made changes too. Personal phone calls and business-class travel had never been condoned, but we understood the need to cut back further. We took pride in being like our leader, Bill Gates, who, at the time, was not only zealous about creating cutting-edge software and beating the competition, but notoriously cheap, wearing clothes from the Gap, and only flying coach.

David and I explored Athens, wandered through the Acropolis and Parthenon, and sat in the sun at outdoor cafes, watching people. We then headed to Mykonos. I hadn't booked accommodations in advance, and when we walked by a hotel with a sweeping view of the Mediterranean and sparkling blue pool, David stopped to ask about rooms.

"We only have one left," the woman at the front desk told us. "It's $180 a night."

Believing the price was too high, I began to back away.

"It's a remodeled windmill that sleeps six," she explained.

"We'll stay three nights," David said.

David hadn't grown up with much money. Unlike me, he didn't view saving as a way to prove his value. His parents had met in Korea where his father, an ROTC scholar, had been serving as a soldier, and his mother, a candy striper, was volunteering in a hospital. Coincidentally, they had both grown up in the Washington, D.C. area, and when they returned to the United States, they did so together, with plans to get married. But neither of their families condoned the union. Nor did the states of Maryland or Virginia. David's father was black, his mother was white, and in 1964, interracial marriage was still illegal in parts of the US.

When David was born, the two families united. But seven years later, David's parents divorced, and David and his younger brother grew up primarily with their single mother. Although David remembered a normal, happy childhood, he also remembered overhearing his mother on the phone, pleading with the neighborhood summer day camp to take him and his brother for free. She needed to go to work and couldn't afford to pay.

When we entered the windmill, David grinned and turned in slow circles, his arms outstretched. I drew in my breath, peeking into one of the downstairs bedrooms, tiptoeing through the kitchen, then making my way up the spiral staircase to the master bedroom.

"Too bad Adam and Lynn, and Donna and Matt aren't with us," I said. "This place is too big for the two of us."

"Yeah, if our friends were here, maybe you could enjoy it," David said.

"I know, I know. What's my problem?" I said. "This is amazing. Here we are on a Greek island, staying in a windmill. Why can't I relax?"

"I don't know. It's not as though you didn't travel as a kid."

"But we didn't travel like this," I argued. "We stayed at inexpensive places."

"You went out to eat too."

"Not very often. Restaurants were for special occasions."

"The first time I went to a restaurant was for my high school graduation," David said.

He then told me about his second experience at a restaurant when he was a summer intern at Citibank during college. As a reward for his good work, his boss had told him to go out for a nice meal. He wasn't accustomed to restaurants and hadn't wanted to spend too much. When he returned with the receipt, his boss told him, "Try again."

"I hadn't spent enough. I never had any money. My life was so different from yours. My brother and I heated up canned spaghetti sauce at home. We ate a lot of Hamburger Helper, the kind with the wagon wheels."

"What's that?" I asked.

"See . . . you lived a privileged life."

"My mom loved to cook," I argued. "She never used Hamburger Helper. Prepackaged, premeasured spices are expensive. It's more economical to cook from scratch."

"It's easy to love to cook if you have time and energy," David countered. "Your mom was home all day. My mom had to work."

"But my mom was very careful with spending," I said defensively.

Somehow, we were trying to outdo one another, David aiming to prove he had grown up with less money and more hardship, and me hoping he knew how frugal I was. Neither of us wanted to be labeled as privileged. Struggling and being careful was more acceptable and respectable than being well-off. After all, the real heroes worked hard, made smart choices, and pulled themselves up by their bootstraps, improving their lot in life.

For years, being cautious with money had given me a sense of purpose, solidifying my place in our family and the world as a responsible person, worthy of my parents' attention and love. When the house felt cold, I knew to put on a sweater. Eating leftovers was praiseworthy too. So was turning off lights when leaving a room. I circled the block in search of free parking on the street, walked as far as necessary to find an ATM that wouldn't charge me a fee, and refused to buy out-of-season raspberries or avocados when the price was too high.

When David and I first started dating, I'd been shocked he hadn't participated in Microsoft's 401K and Employee Stock Purchase plans. I couldn't imagine why someone who had just graduated from business school wasn't taking advantage of those opportunities. Microsoft matched a percentage of what employees contributed. Not investing was like throwing money away.

"You need to sign up," I'd told him.

"With student loans and car payments, I wasn't sure I'd have enough money to set aside," he said.

Thinking about the money David owed for school and about

his lack of experience putting money in the bank, I couldn't deny my childhood had been more privileged than his. In fact, my childhood seemed to have been more privileged than I'd realized, perhaps more privileged than either of my parents acknowledged or understood. Even though my father had been successful, he was still afraid of not having enough to eat. And concerned with propriety, my mother watched her spending. I too was stuck in the past, adhering to old habits and beliefs, being careful with money even when watching every penny no longer made sense—if it ever had.

By our third night in Mykonos, I had fallen in love with our windmill. It was wonderful to have so much room to spread out and fun to sleep in such a historic place. We even considered staying a fourth night. But, excited to visit other islands, we boarded a ferry to Naxos where we hiked through the countryside for a couple of days. We then continued onward to Santorini, disembarked at the port, and made our way up the hill. And when we spotted a beautiful, three-star hotel with an open-air lobby full of flowering plants and colorful tiles, we booked ourselves a room, changed into swimsuits, and headed to the pool. Sinking into a blue-cushioned lounge chair, David opened his book while I abandoned myself to *The Bridges of Madison County*—it was vacation, after all.

An hour later, I looked up.

"Let's go for a walk," I said.

"I want to finish this chapter," David replied.

Looking back down at my book, I couldn't get comfortable. It didn't feel right to be lazing around doing nothing, especially at an expensive hotel. For years, I'd looked down on the self-indulgent behavior of lounging around. I didn't want to be one of *those people* who visited foreign countries but never ventured outside their exclusive, high-end resorts. If my parents had been in Greece, they wouldn't have been sitting by the pool. They'd have been out seeing sights, making every second count. They wouldn't have said as much aloud, but they would have been trying to make every dollar count too.

The next morning, after sleeping in late and lingering over breakfast, David and I finally left the hotel. But we didn't get far. At the end of the street, David stopped abruptly in front of a row of open-topped jeeps.

"Cool," he said. "Let's drive to the other side of the island."

"Why don't we just look around here?"

Even as my brain reminded me of my desire to enjoy the vacation, my gut churned, my heels dug in, and my first-grade self began to throw a tantrum. We couldn't just hop in a jeep. They were so overpriced. We didn't need to drive around. We were already in Greece, living extravagantly. Why did David always have to push things too far?

"These jeeps are rip-offs," I said. "They're taking advantage of tourists."

"Who cares?" David said. "They look fun."

In the end, I swallowed my upset and we were soon bouncing along a dirt road, past vineyards and secluded beaches to the far side of the island. We stopped in a town perched on the cliffs and wandered the narrow streets, admiring the whitewashed buildings and blue of the sea. In the evening, we watched the oranges and pinks of the sunset fade to darkness from a rooftop bar—and that upset resurfaced. No switch had flipped. No magic had happened. My attitude wasn't more relaxed. I wasn't more carefree. Even though I was on vacation in Greece with my boyfriend, my past was still present. My childhood habits and beliefs remained. I was worried about being responsible, upset about all the money we'd spent. A million dollars hadn't changed everything or made my life perfect. All that money didn't seem nearly as powerful as I'd always believed.

Contemplation & Conversation

- What assumptions, emotions, and thoughts about money were part of your childhood? What beliefs have you let go of? What have you held onto?

- What was your first money memory? What emotions were attached?

- Jennifer hears her mother's voice when she's thinking about flying business class. Do your parents approve of the way you handle money? Do they still influence how you think about finances?

Chapter Three

HOUSES

n the mid-1990s, Microsoft employees were working as hard as ever and the stock price was soaring. But a shift had occurred. People were taking more notice of their growing net worth. Some were setting work phones to speed dial the information-line at the *Seattle Times* for up-to-the-minute stock quotes. Others were creating spreadsheets behind closed office doors. When plugging the day's stock price into a personalized grid indicated hundreds of thousands of dollars had been made in a week, it was hard not to take notice—and rejoice. In fact, celebrations were beginning to spill into the halls. A guy on our test team had started blowing a horn every time the stock price went up a dollar, and many days, it sounded like quitting time every hour.

Not only were employees tracking their skyrocketing wealth and becoming increasingly vocal about their good fortune, many were spending big. A few outliers had been driving Lamborghinis and Ferraris for years, but a whole new crop of Pathfinders, Miatas, and Saabs was showing up in the parking lots. Employees in their late twenties and early thirties were buying houses too, snapping up new-construction monstrosities in the suburbs around Redmond and purchasing places in Seattle normally reserved for the well-established.

With so many employees cashing in, when David and I attended a party at the new home of a software developer in his group, neither of us was surprised to be knocking on the door of a French château. Within a gated community, boasting a turret, the house was not our style, but Rick, the owner, was pleased. He welcomed us inside and for a few awkward moments, the three of us stood in the foyer, Rick looking out of place in his cutoff shorts, and me gazing up at the vaulted three-story ceiling and crystal chandelier.

"Come in, join the party," Rick finally said.

He showed us into the kitchen, past gleaming granite countertops and an eight-burner stove, and through an expansive family room. We continued toward the back and onto a sprawling wooden deck, our footsteps echoing off the hardwood floors and cream-colored walls. Except for a college futon, some pillows, and a few empty Domino's pizza boxes on the floor, the house was empty.

"That's weird," I said to David on our drive home.

Just as I'd been surprised by the home of Bill Gates, I was mystified by Rick's place. Why was someone with so much money sitting on the floor, eating pizza out of boxes? I thought the rich were all leading spectacular lives in elegantly decorated, well-maintained homes. But I was learning that millions of dollars didn't necessarily lead a person to start living a glamorous lifestyle. Money didn't impart good taste or an interest in interior design, and didn't come with a how-to manual, either.

Like many at Microsoft in 1994, Donna and Matt were

cashing in options. Recently engaged and preparing for a life together, they had sold Matt's 900-square-foot bungalow and purchased a 4,000-square-foot house with five bedrooms, four bathrooms, and a panoramic view of Lake Washington. Their house was incredible—and clearly not the norm for most young couples who were just starting out. Similarly, Lynn and Adam, who had recently become husband and wife, had just purchased an Arts and Crafts home on a high-end street. Meanwhile, David and I were still renting two separate apartments, lugging clothes and milk from one to the other.

With our friends having made the move from renting to owning, I shouldn't have been surprised when David announced he wanted to buy a house. But my feelings were hurt. A house was a big step. Weren't we a team? Why was he considering such a big purchase without first consulting me? Then, seeing the mischievous look in his eyes, believing he just wanted to have some fun, when he suggested we go house hunting together, I agreed to play along.

Just three years earlier, working in advertising, counting every penny, scraping together rent, I would never have even thought to look at houses. Like most single women in their mid-twenties in Seattle, I couldn't have afforded to buy one. But with Microsoft options, surrounded by friends and co-workers who were spending big, it sounded reasonable to shop for a house. It also sounded like fun.

Breezing past the cemented relationship status our friends had achieved, David and I talked about the houses they had chosen. We liked the character and charm of Donna and Matt's place and wanted to be within walking distance of shops and restaurants like Lynn and Adam. With our friends' homes our benchmarks, we strolled through our neighborhood, looking for a first home—nothing too big or too small, but something just right for a nice, young, professional couple.

Seeing a huge, turn-of-the-century house with FOR SALE signs on the front lawn, we walked up the front path, and in the open door. Why not take a look? The entry was grand, with high, plaster ceilings and dark hardwood floors. A carved mahogany staircase on our left circled up to a second floor. To the right, the living room boasted leaded-glass windows and stately antiques. Under different circumstances, I might have looked over at David, thinking "if only" or "maybe someday." As it was, I had no interest. Our stock options allowed us to purchase the house outright in cash, but I wasn't considering the freedom we had to pick and choose, or contemplating our privilege, musing about how nice it was to have money. Quite the opposite. I didn't see myself as rich and didn't want any-thing big and flashy. My ideal first home was a small, cozy place that would take time to fix up, requiring my husband and me to paint, put up wallpaper, and spend weekends at home improve-ment stores. I'd long imagined a first home as a project, a shared goal, and a way to build a life together. David and I weren't fifty years old. We weren't a family of five. We weren't even engaged. A half-million-dollar house was completely incongruous with who we were, how we lived, and my vision.

As if to verify we were in completely the wrong place, a real-tor in a tailored white suit and tasteful heels, her blonde hair perfectly coiffed and pulled back in a bun, entered the room. Her eyes slid from our jeans to our tennis shoes as she gave us an obligatory welcome, telling us she needed to go outside to arrange her signs. Looking around, noting a Louis Vuitton purse on a chair and pegging her as the owner of the silver Mercedes sedan out front, as she dismissed us, I dismissed her too. She looked typical of the rich: obnoxious, arrogant, and image-conscious. I'd learned about people like her from visiting my grandparents at their place on Lake Michigan.

When my mother was a girl, she spent vacations at her family's cottage in Wequetonsing, a summer community three hours from where she lived in Flint. She'd loved sailing with her father and swimming in the lake. But when I was a girl and our family visited Wequetonsing, my mother had seemed ill at ease in the upper-class surroundings. As we walked along the lakefront, looking at the three- and four-story houses, she whispered about the inhabitants being very well-to-do.

"They're sipping cocktails and waiting to be served," she said.

Then, as though holding a dirty rag at arm's length, disgusted but unable to let go, she pointed to one of the largest houses and told me the help lived in the back.

One evening, when my grandfather took our family out for dinner, my mother got us all gussied up. My father wore his work suit. Michael had his hair slicked to one side. I put on a dress, frilly white anklets, and black Mary Janes. With my mother calling the restaurant fancy and my grandparents declaring it elegant, I knew to be on my best behavior, to mind my p's and q's, and not to order anything too expensive. I was probably scanning the right-hand side of the menu, searching for the smallest numbers rather than considering what I wanted to eat, when my grandfather stood up and put his napkin on the table. A man and a woman dressed for a party had entered the dining room and were gliding in our direction. When they reached our table, everyone stood. I watched as my grandparents chatted with their friends and introduced them to my parents, wondering if the couple was royalty of some sort. Maybe they were famous. The honey of their voices and elegance they exuded filled the space around us.

When the glowing man and woman departed, we sat down. A shadow fell, the room went gray, and my grandparents leaned in toward the center of the table.

"He's never worked," my grandfather said, his voice low.

"They are such lovely people," my grandmother added, a smile frozen on her face. "They're very generous people."

"They have a big home on the lake," my grandfather said. "He likes to golf. You know how *those people* spend their time."

The tone of my grandfather's voice and the look on his face confused me. Only over time did I come to understand the influence of the Great Depression. After living through financially difficult years, my grandparents had learned to watch every penny. They had also become resentful of the moneyed classes and their morally bankrupt ways. As my grandmother snuck Saltines from restaurant tables and stashed them in her purse, pleased to have a snack tucked away for later, "Just in case," she kept her rich friends at a cautious distance, like exotic animals in the zoo.

One late afternoon, when I was a teen, my mother picked me up from a friend's house.

"Did you have fun?" she asked.

"It was great! Have you been in their living room?"

My mother shook her head.

"It's so pretty. There's a big fireplace, white sofas, matching chairs. They only use it for guests. Kids aren't supposed to go in. But we did. And we played Ping-Pong and foosball in the basement."

"I'm glad you had a good time," my mother said, curtly.

"Mrs. Roberts took us to their country club. We rode in the back of the station wagon and swam in the pool."

My mother gripped the steering wheel and stared ahead.

"Mrs. Roberts made cookies," I said. "They have a microwave in their kitchen. And an electric can opener."

We pulled to an abrupt stop in front of Dip'n Donuts.

"Do you want a donut?" my mother asked. "Or maybe these aren't good enough. Does Mrs. Roberts make her own?"

I was quiet as my mother continued.

"I'm glad we aren't living in that type of neighborhood anymore. We couldn't have afforded that country club or kept up with *those people*," she said. "You've always been so interested in money."

My mother's reaction hurt. She seemed jealous of Mrs. Roberts—and dismayed by me. I was ashamed of what she perceived to be my interest in money. After all, responsible girls weren't supposed to care about material things.

Standing in the large, turn-of-the-century house, watching the realtor turn her back and walk out the door to arrange her signs, I wanted to run. I didn't want to be anything like my grandparents' friends or a daughter who was interested in auspiciously large houses.

"Let's go," I said to David.

Driving to a more down-to-earth neighborhood, we stopped outside a small white bungalow with a FOR SALE sign in the front. Inside, a guy in his late twenties was sitting on a folding metal chair, reading a book. He stood when we entered, introduced himself as James, then gave us a tour. Although the house wasn't quite what either of us wanted, we asked James to be our buyer's agent.

I was interested in a home that fit with how I saw myself. I was practical too. With the Microsoft stock price soaring, it was wisest to hold onto our options and let their value grow. So, when James asked about our budget, David and I told him we wanted to spend between $150,000 and $180,000, an amount we could easily afford on our salaries, which would get us a decent-sized fixer-upper in a comfortable neighborhood and wouldn't require cashing in options.

But then, when James took us to look at houses, we stood on the sidewalk in front of the first place he wanted to show us, and didn't go in. The house wasn't welcoming. I stared at the peeling paint on the front and the cracked concrete stairs leading up to the door and, suddenly, owning a fixer-upper didn't seem romantic. Hearing traffic from the nearby highway, I thought of Donna and Matt, and Lynn and Adam, and the places they'd purchased. Were David and I on the path to repeating our San Francisco weekend experience in the form of a house? We didn't *need* to buy a starter home. We didn't need to spend time at home improvement stores or hanging wall-paper either. Even if we didn't cash in options, we could afford to purchase a place that didn't require so much work and was still in keeping with who we were—or at least in keeping with who I'd always been and imagined myself to be.

"You know," David said, turning to James, "I don't think we need to go in."

"It's cozy inside . . . and much nicer than it looks from the street," James countered.

We shook our heads.

Driving to the next location, James talked about imagination and vision. Sure enough, we needed both. The owners had made many of their own improvements, adding a porch out back that looked too unstable to use, and a greenhouse in the master bedroom that made the whole place smell of dirt. David and I walked through in silence, shooting looks at each other behind James' back.

"I think we should spend a bit more," I said once we were alone.

"Yeah, we need to double our budget," David said.

I froze at the suggestion. My identity was at stake. We were a young professional couple working our way up. It didn't feel right to suddenly double our budget. Who could do such a thing?

"What will James think?" I said.

"He'll probably think, 'better commission for me,'" David said.

"But he'll look at us differently," I said.

I wanted James to like us, not think we were cavalier with

our money. I certainly didn't want him to think we had a lot of it.

"It's James's job to find us a house," David said. "We're his clients."

David had a point. James was our buyer's agent. But our rapport was so good. If we doubled our budget, I was afraid he'd see us as people with whom he couldn't relate, with whom he had nothing in common. Would he think of us as obnoxious? I didn't want him to think we were people to keep at a distance like my grandparents' friends—people who were rich. I didn't want to think of myself that way either.

David said he had no problem telling James we were interested in places in a higher price range, so I let him do the talking. But when we went out again to look at houses with James, it was clear David hadn't told him we wanted to double our budget. The next house we saw was a Tudor listed for $220,000 with a tall pine tree out front, a large deck in the back, and three small bedrooms upstairs. Walking through the living room, admiring the hardwood floors and old-fashioned tiled fireplace, the private glances David and I exchanged were altogether different. The house wasn't too big or too small. It felt just right for a young professional couple.

As we walked to the car, David reached for my hand.

"I can imagine living there," he said. "With you."

Suddenly, I didn't know how to respond. What was I doing? I didn't want to buy a house just because we could afford one. It wasn't about the money. We'd found an ideal first house, but a home was more about building a life together than about making a purchase. I didn't want to live with David unless we had a plan for the future—*our* future.

"That deck will be great for eating outside in the summer," David continued.

"I don't want a house," I blurted out.

David stopped. He looked hurt. But he recovered quickly.

"I'll buy it," he said. "You can live with me."

I saw David's grin. Then all I saw were his teeth, big and white. I looked away, blinking.

"I like the house," my voice said. "But it brings up questions. I don't want to just live together. I want to be with *you*."

"Me too," David said, finally aware I was upset. "I want to be with you too."

I didn't know how to say what I wanted. David didn't seem to be catching on. I wished he'd figure it out, and want the same himself. As it was, he was just bulldozing along, playing around, doing whatever caught his interest, trying to have it all without considering me—or us. We had stock options and loads of freedom, but my ideal first home wasn't something money could buy.

Contemplation & Conversation

- What stereotypes of wealth and the wealthy do you believe hold true? Why?

- Jennifer doesn't want to see herself as someone with money. Does the amount of money you have affect how you see yourself? How others see you?

- How does where you live reflect who you are and what you value? Is your home an accurate reflection of your financial situation?

Chapter Four

TRUTH SERUM

In the fall of 1994, over three years after David and I met at Microsoft, I arrived at his apartment and rang the bell, looking forward to taking him out for dinner to celebrate the success of a presentation he'd given at work.

"You're here," he said, finally opening the door, looking uncharacteristically ready to go.

David's face was clean-shaven, his white shirt pressed, and he was wearing the brown and black houndstooth sports jacket we'd dubbed "the professor" for its tweedy, intellectual quality. It could have had suede patches on the elbows, but thankfully did not.

"Are you ready?" I asked. "Everything okay?"

"Yes. Fine. Let's go," he said, but seemed in a daze.

As we drove to the restaurant, I detected Racquet Club cologne, a scent David's grandmother had given him for his twelfth birthday, which he used sparingly for special occasions. He'd clearly gotten dressed up.

When we were close to the restaurant, I circled the block, scanning for parking, and seeing a flash of taillights, a free spot just a block away, I knew it was our lucky night. We entered the restaurant, and right away, the host led us through the peach-colored dining room, directly to a table near the window. After sitting down, we studied our menus, the aroma of herbs and red wine drifting over from the open kitchen where a wood burning oven blazed. Everything sounded delicious. There was duck breast with port and cherries, wild mushroom risotto, a pan-seared salmon with huckleberry sauce. Mulling over the choices, I was surprised when the host appeared at our table with a bottle of champagne. How did he know we were celebrating? I smiled and nodded, watching him remove the foil at the top of the bottle. He gave the wire a few quick twists, slowly loosened the cork, and with a festive pop and a skillful pour, two tall flutes stood before us.

"Congratulations," I said, lifting my glass. "Tell me how it went. What questions did people ask?"

David took a long sip of champagne. Returning his glass to the table, he wiped his mouth with his twisted napkin and glanced around the room.

"I actually have . . ." he said, leaning over the table, attempting to find something in his jacket pocket. "I have something I want to ask you."

He pushed back his chair and, holding a small blue velvet box in one hand and opening it with the other, he lowered himself to one knee.

"Will you marry me?" he asked.

For a moment, I just stared, the room becoming a peachy blur. It was the question I'd wanted to hear, but I was surprised.

"Yes. Yes," I said, tugging at David's sleeve to get him to stand. Standing myself, I threw my arms around his neck in a clumsy embrace, giving him a quick kiss, and then another and another, telling him how much I loved him.

As we sat down, I looked at the ring in its box.

"I'm so surprised . . . and so happy. When did you do this?"

"This afternoon," David said. "Wait. Did you say yes?"

"Yes! Of course, I said yes."

Song filled the room. The restaurant's owner was walking in our direction, serenading us with opera, his voice booming, his arms outstretched. All the other diners had stopped talking. They were looking at us, smiling. Some began to clap.

When the song ended and people returned to their meals, David leaned over our table, grabbed my hands, and pulled me toward him.

"I'm so glad you said yes," he whispered. "I was so nervous. Can you feel that? My hands are shaking."

"Did you think I'd say no?"

"I knew you'd say yes, but—I didn't. I haven't done this before."

Earlier that afternoon, David had called my parents to ask for my hand in marriage, earning himself big points with my mother and father. Having secured their blessing, he raced downtown to a jeweler's, arriving fifteen minutes before the store closed to choose a ring. On the way home, he'd stopped at the restaurant to reserve our special spot by the window.

"So that's why he brought champagne. You did a lot in a couple of hours. That was a quick ring purchase."

"This doesn't have to be the ring you keep," David informed me. "Do you like it?"

I took the ring from the box, placed it on my finger and held out my hand, examining the diamond at arm's length as David watched. The setting was just what I would have chosen myself: simple and classic with a round gem floating in a white-gold band—but was the diamond a bit too small?

I hadn't been aware of a desire to marry Prince Charming, but getting engaged was like being in a fairytale. The man I loved had asked me to marry him. I was thrilled to think of David as my husband, me his wife. For weeks, nothing bothered me. I smiled while waiting in line, shrugged when late, and regaled co-workers at Microsoft with the story of the proposal. I also called old friends from high school and college and spent hours on the phone with my mother, sharing my excitement. She was my best listener, pleased David would be her son-in-law, and happier still to know her thirty-year-old daughter would finally be getting married.

But while I smiled through each day, happy to be engaged, I was increasingly plagued by an unpleasant, shameful desire. I wanted a bigger diamond—and was horrified to care. Until David held that blue velvet box before me, I hadn't given engagement rings a moment of thought. Expensive baubles and jewels had never been my daydreams. Then again, I'd loved the strand of pink-white pearls my parents had given me for my twenty-first birthday. I'd worn that necklace with pride during my senior year of college, believing it made me part of the in-crowd. All the East Coast girls had pearls. But what was going on now? Was I looking for the right ring to replace my coed necklace, hoping to fit in? Had I grown up at all? Was I so insecure? Was I *that* shallow and materialistic?

For days, I wrestled with myself, uncomfortable about my wish for a larger gem and unsure why I cared—and my diamond took on a sinister life of its own. I did my best to scold it into submission with a firm "down boy" and wag of a finger, telling it size didn't matter. But my little diamond was so demanding. It wouldn't leave me alone. Worse still, other diamonds joined in, ganging up against me, showing off as bigger, bolder, and brighter than my own, glistening from the fingers of strangers in the street, and beckoning from offices at work.

"Can I see your ring?" I asked a woman at Microsoft. "It's so pretty."

I held her fingers and looked for as long as was polite.

"Thank you," she cooed. "I'm happy. He did a good job."

I wanted to grab her hand and pull it close to my face, to get a long, hard look at exactly how her diamond compared. Why was it so much bigger than mine?

I knew, intellectually, that the heft of my diamond didn't add to my value and had nothing to do with the depth of David's love. The size was not a reflection of the importance he placed on our relationship either. He didn't care about diamonds. Was his money to blame? He had so much of it, more than I could fathom, more than was comfortable to contemplate. If the possibility of a bigger diamond hadn't existed, if those stock options hadn't seemed to be demanding something big, I probably wouldn't have been dreaming of more sparkle. Not me. I wasn't *that* girl. And yet, with the stock price soaring, with David having been promoted—twice—he could afford a diamond of any size. If the stock price continued climbing, in the next couple of years, he would have nearly ten million dollars. Ten million dollars! It was an astronomical amount. Ten million dollars demanded a bigger diamond.

But, ashamed to be thinking about David's stock options, and even more mortified by my craving for bling, I didn't say anything. How could I tell him I was thinking about money and worried my diamond was too small? I couldn't possibly make such a horrifying confession. Luckily, David brought up the subject of my ring himself, telling me that before asking for my hand in marriage, he had called Matt for advice on buying a ring. Then, after learning Donna's diamond was "about a carat," he'd visited a jeweler and purchased a .93-carat diamond for $3,500.

"Let's go back to the jeweler and look around," he said. "I didn't know what I was doing."

Dashing to the car, I told myself it only made sense to do a little shopping. I'd be wearing my ring every day for the rest of my life. Neither of us knew anything about diamonds. We needed to educate ourselves.

Before entering the jeweler's, I pulled David to a stop in front of the store window and pointed to a yellow diamond pendant the size and shape of an almond. Pronouncing it rare, I turned, almost bumping into the guard by the door. For a moment, I was afraid he might reach out and stop me. Could he tell I was an imposter, attempting to access a world about which I knew nothing? Was he aware of me being an unlikable character, dissatisfied with my ring, and hoping my fiancé would buy me something bigger? But he barely glanced in my direction as we stepped inside.

We made our way toward the back and my attention was

drawn to a case filled with jewels. Mesmerized, I leaned over the glass to get a better look at a pair of emerald earrings, glad David couldn't see me visualizing myself as their owner. All the gems in the case were so beautiful, so dazzling. My eyes slid to the right, landing on a diamond bracelet before catching sight of a saleswoman who was shifting in our direction.

"You took your time," she said to David. "But I knew you'd be back."

The saleswoman was only a few years older than me, but her smile was as practiced as someone twice my age.

"He was here just a couple minutes and paid full price," she informed me.

I forced a smile as David told her we were interested in seeing a few more diamonds.

"Perfect," she purred.

She paraded us to the back of the store where we exited through a door into a startlingly bright room.

"Please, have a seat," she said, pointing to two chairs in front of a large wooden desk. "May I see your ring?"

She lifted a grey velvet cloth out of a drawer and smoothed it flat with the palm of a manicured hand. Then, holding my ring between her thumb and index finger, with a monocle to her eye, she disappeared behind a waterfall of blonde hair.

"Our clients bring in their old pieces when they are ready to upgrade," her voice declared. "You can make exchanges any time. When it comes to engagement rings, everyone buys the biggest diamond they can afford."

She set the ring down and looked directly at David, who

seemed completely immune to her salesmanship. She then turned her smile on me.

"When he gets promoted and you want a bigger diamond, you can always come back. What you get today is not what you'll want ten years from now."

I was both intrigued and disgusted, ashamed of my greed and newfound interest in sparkle. Her statement was distasteful. Yet, I was wishing for a bigger diamond that very same day. The saleswomen pulled a black box out of a drawer and opened the lid. Using long silver tweezers, she removed several icy gems and placed them gently on the velvet. She then handed me my ring along with a loupe and explained the meaning of cut, color, and clarity. What a shock! Size wasn't the only problem. There were defects everywhere. Hundreds of scratches, squiggles, and blemishes snaked through the diamond in my ring.

Staring helplessly at the flaws, as they jeered back at me, I sat silently in my shame, unable to admit the truth to myself let alone to my fiancé. How could I confess to craving a bigger, flawless, colorless, perfectly-cut stone?

"What do you think?" I heard him ask. "Do you like any of these?"

To David, the attributes of a diamond were as meaningless as the dictate to spend two month's salary on a ring. He knew it was all a ploy orchestrated by De Beers. Logically, I knew it too. But De Beers had seduced me—and many others. In 1940, before De Beers launched a campaign linking diamonds to engagement, only ten percent of brides-to-be wore a ring with a diamond. Then, after De Beers began generating demand, asserting that two months' salary was a small price to pay, capitalizing on a woman's interest in romance, and promising a diamond was forever, by 1990, eighty percent of all new brides had diamonds in their engagement rings.

But De Beers wasn't the only reason for my interest in more sparkle. Our wealth was egging me on too. Just as De Beers had added diamonds to the American collective unconscious as the symbol of forever, for years, Hollywood had been showing me how the rich were supposed to live. Whether flashy or elegant, garish or sophisticated, rich people needed to look the part, and my look was sorely lacking.

"Just ask," Wealth scoffed. "You don't know how to live. What a waste. You aren't cultured or savvy enough to have money. You'll never fit in or have the appropriate style."

Although she had no idea how much money we had, in my head, my mother chimed in too, calling down from above.

"Where is this shallow interest coming from?" she asked. "What have I done wrong? Do you really want something showy and ostentatious? You've always cared too much about material things."

She was right, of course. Huge diamonds were for spoiled princesses and my mother's worst nightmare. Her ring was tasteful, a band with a subtle row of five tiny diamonds. She wasn't one of *those people* flaunting a rock.

"Do you like this one?" David asked.

I shifted in my chair as the room began to spin and the gems danced on their velvet bed.

"Any of these are good," I said.

"Good? What do you mean 'good'?"

David sounded annoyed, but I couldn't answer. I couldn't

look in his direction. I wanted my fiancé to choose a bigger diamond, hop in the Jeep, and save me from my shame. But diamonds weren't David's toys, and since he didn't think to play the knight, we ended up leaving the store with the same ring we had brought in.

During the months that followed, I was too busy at work to think much about my ring. Our team was preparing to launch *Utopia* and expectations were high. Upper management believed the product would be a huge success, giving home users a whole new way of interacting with their computers to accomplish tasks. We'd hired an outside agency to come up with the name *Microsoft Bob*. We'd also convinced Bill Gates to unveil *Bob* at the 1995 Consumer Electronics Show in Las Vegas. But the unique name and fanfare only turned our product into a more spectacular flop. The animated characters meant to help people write letters, track finances, and organize their schedules didn't revolutionize home computing. Focusing on the user interface, we'd failed to recognize the product we had: software that only appealed to new users and required hardware way beyond the capacity of most home machines. Luckily, at Microsoft and within the tech industry in general, risks and failures were viewed as opportunities to learn.

As I was doing a lot of learning from *Microsoft Bob*, I was also planning our wedding—designing invitations with Donna, selecting flowers with my mother, and doing most everything else with David. The two of us toured potential venues for the reception. We also listened to bands and tasted cakes. Our goal was to create a festive atmosphere with delicious food and lots of dancing. The wedding ceremony was important too. Since David had grown up Episcopalian, we attended classes and went through premarital counseling, which brought us closer.

When our wedding preparations were complete and my frenzied days at work had grown calmer, I gathered my courage.

"I feel bad about this," I said, standing in front of the mirror in David's bedroom. "I've wanted to tell you for a while but couldn't admit it to myself."

His face appeared in the mirror behind me.

"What is it?" he asked.

Seeing the worry in his eyes, I turned quickly and wrapped my arms around him, holding tight.

"Oh, it's nothing," I said into his shoulder.

After a few moments, David pulled away and stared at me, again asking what was wrong.

"It's just . . . my ring," I said. "I'd like to get a platinum band. The white gold doesn't show off the diamond."

He laughed. "Is that all?"

I nodded, pulled him close, and hid my face in his chest.

◆　◆　◆

Over Labor Day weekend, on September 2, 1995, wearing my mother's raw silk wedding dress, my father walking me down the aisle, I met David at the altar. Surrounded by family and friends, we became husband and wife. After the ceremony, we were chauffeured in an antique Rolls Royce to the Seattle Art Museum where we celebrated in the open front lobby, David looking handsome in his tuxedo, and me deeply content. The smart, funny man by my side, who made me feel seen and understood, was my forever partner. Together, we cut into a two-tiered white cake decorated with blue delphiniums and waltzed to Anne Murray's "Could I Have This Dance."

Although my father and I never spoke directly about the costs, he underwrote our big day, happy to do so. He was probably also relieved David and I covered extra expenses, happy to do so as well. We were lucky we could contribute and not worry about prices. Just as De Beers influenced my desire for a diamond, I'd been convinced that no expense should be spared for a couple's once-in-a-lifetime special day. Big-ticket items like venue, catering, and band seemed like necessary expenses, out of my control. But when it came to smaller costs, I wasn't carefree.

After saving my pennies and working for $3.25 an hour in the summers during high school, I understood the value of a dollar. So, when my father generously gave us cases of wine made from the grapes he'd grown and the caterer wanted to charge us $5 per bottle for corkage, I was outraged. Five dollars was way too much to pay to drink our own wine. But instead of wasting energy in anger, I played a trick in my mind, telling myself that I was paying a flat $300 fee to have my father's wine poured all evening long for our guests.

In years to come, both David and I would continue to find spending small more psychologically difficult than spending big. It was relatively easy to pay an exorbitant amount on a hotel room than to buy anything from the minibar. To David, minibar pricing was illogical. To me, it was a rip-off. Even when spending thousands on accommodations, neither of us could bring ourselves to pay $6 for a small bottle of water.

For our honeymoon, David and I flew to Portugal, spent several days exploring Lisbon, then continued south to the island of Madeira where we checked into a gorgeous hilltop hotel overlooking a lush valley and the Mediterranean Sea. The setting was idyllic. But standing on our balcony, the second evening of our stay, watching the hotel staff set up for dinner in the garden below, I wanted to cry. When I'd suggested we eat outside at the hotel, David had groaned. He wasn't in the mood. He didn't want yet another elaborate meal. He wanted to order room service—and despite the tranquility and appearance of perfection, I felt a rising panic.

Over the previous days, David had been right about everything. He knew how to read a map and which museums to visit. He'd taken to criticizing me too, suggesting various improvements I needed to make, like spending less time getting ready in the evenings and being less particular about where we ate. Now, because of my interest in dining in the garden, I wasn't giving us enough downtime. Obviously, he said, we should eat something simple in the room. We'd been out every night. It was time to stay in.

Looking over at my husband as he lay on the bed reading, I couldn't stop the tears. Caught up in the wedding, choosing a band, selecting a menu, hoping to make the evening perfect, I'd lost track of our relationship. Did David see and accept me? Did I accept him?

"Have we made a mistake?" I finally asked.

In many ways, I'd set myself up. My expectations around honeymoons had me imagining nothing but romantic nights full of candlelit dinners, the two of us gazing into one another's eyes after long glorious days of togetherness, walks on long sandy beaches, holding hands, deep in meaningful conversation, me beautiful and smiling, David handsome and adoring. The fact that we were honeymooning in Europe, staying in beautiful hotels, made it seem even more critical to feel nothing but perfectly content. How could I not? And yet, no matter what our circumstances, no matter where we were, even though we were married, we were still ourselves—two separate people with messy emotions and thoughts of our own.

That night, David and I spent time listening to one another. As we allowed ourselves to be vulnerable, we again felt the love that existed between us. While I'd felt criticized and inadequate, David had been feeling unacknowledged and unheard. He'd taken my slowness in the evenings and my focus on food as a sign of me not caring about him or his feelings.

Decades later, we would discuss that evening again, and to my complete surprise, David would admit he'd been worried about money. He had upgraded us to a nicer room overlooking the garden, then, unbeknownst to me, he'd begun to think about how much we were spending.

"We paid a lot for the wedding. The honeymoon was expensive. When we upgraded to that room, I felt as though we were out of control," he told me. "I didn't want to pay more for that dinner."

"I had no idea! Spending has never been an issue for you. Why didn't you tell me?"

"I was a new husband," he said. "I wasn't going to admit being worried about finances to my new wife."

"But I was in tears," I said. "I thought there was some big problem between us. You should have said something. I had no idea."

I'd hoped for the perfect honeymoon, a special wedding, and the right diamond for my engagement ring. Clearly, David had had expectations too. He'd wanted to be in charge, to have everything go smoothly, and to be on top of our finances, making our honeymoon special. Even with me crying and upset, fearing we'd made a mistake, he'd kept his financial concerns to himself.

"It probably would have been healthier if I'd said something," David admitted.

"I think it would have brought us closer," I said. "As it was, I was worried about our relationship. Plus, you were holding that burden. I didn't even have the opportunity to share it with you."

Over the years, David and I have become better communicators. We've learned to talk through tough times and hard emotions and have been keeping the conversation going. While money has made our life easier, talking about finances and being in sync with our values and goals has been important too. The amount we have hasn't been as instrumental to our happiness as agreeing on when, where, and how much to spend and to save—and talking when we don't.

◆　◆　◆

Like the call I'd gotten from Donna five years earlier letting me know about an opening at Microsoft, in 1996 David got a call that would lead to a pivotal decision. A guy named Jeff Bezos was conducting a reference-check for a VP of Marketing candidate who was a friend of David's. After forty-five minutes, they were still talking. A few weeks after that, David and I found ourselves having dinner with Jeff and his wife, MacKenzie.

The four of us sat around a small table, sampled fried sage leaves, and shared courtship stories. We also discussed the business Jeff was running out of his garage. At the end of the evening, David and I were looking forward to seeing Jeff and MacKenzie again. But our attention turned first to life's next big step. I hadn't grown up dreaming of motherhood, but at thirty-one years old, married to David, I was excited about starting a family. David wanted to have children too, and it wasn't long before we were counting weeks and consulting *What to Expect When You're Expecting*.

In November, we went out with Jeff and MacKenzie again. This time, as we chatted over pasta, Jeff told us more about his company, Amazon.com. He also mentioned his search for a new marketing VP. And as David and I made our way to the car, I wondered aloud if he might be interested in the job.

In 1996, no one was leaving Microsoft. A few employees had begun complaining about the "golden handcuffs" of their unvested stock options, their future fortunes keeping them tied to the company. Others were talking of "resting and vesting," coasting along until they could cash in their options. But David was still fully engaged—and curious about Jeff's company.

David had long been a reader. As a young boy, he was often staring at a book, walking to school, lost in a story, prompting neighbors to call his mother, worried about him crossing the street. In high school, his love for technology led him to spend hours in RadioShack writing programs on the demonstration TRS-80 with his best friend. And, as an adult, curious about the bookstore Jeff was building on the internet, David wanted to learn more. After talking with Jeff, then going through a series of interviews, he had a decision to make.

"Jeff doesn't want to hire me for marketing," David told me, pacing the kitchen. "But he created a vice president of product development position and offered me the job."

"Amazon is just getting started," I said. "It's a great time to join. You could have a huge impact."

David agreed. But when he tried to give notice at Microsoft, a commotion ensued. Upper management did everything possible to convince him to stay, presenting him with opportunities, benefits, and money. Not only did Microsoft offer him one hundred thousand stock options, Steve Ballmer, Bill Gate's second-in-command, called David into his office, apoplectic at the thought of his departure.

"He'd just gotten off a plane from Japan and must have been exhausted," David told me. "But he was manic. For an hour, he yelled at me as he bounced a basketball on the floor of his office."

David met with Bill Gates too.

"Bill told me leaving Microsoft would be the stupidest decision I'd ever make," David said.

"Maybe he has a point," I said.

Microsoft was highly successful and David's career was on a fast track. After working as a summer intern on Access and being hired into the group full-time, he'd advanced quickly. He had over one hundred people working for him and had recently been chosen to create and manage a new finance product. With Bill applying pressure to get him to stay, was leaving the company a good decision? Jeff might be ambitious, with plans to build a billion-dollar business, but startups were a lot of work. We were about to have a baby. Was a new job in a bookstore, playing with technology a good idea when Microsoft was doing so well and we were going to be parents?

"I'm not sure about the timing," I said. "You'll want to be with the baby."

"I'll get plenty of paternity leave and vacation time," David said. "But I agree. Most people are telling me to stay at Microsoft, telling me to 'have one baby at a time'."

"What about all those Microsoft options?" I said. "Did they really offer you one hundred thousand options? That could be worth twenty or thirty million dollars—or more."

In just a couple of years, David would have ten million dollars, an amount beyond anything I'd ever imagined. And yet, strangely, after several months of living with the idea, ten million dollars no longer sounded outrageous. In fact, as I thought about the twenty or thirty million dollars David had been offered, ten million dollars didn't sound like that much. Amounts were surprisingly relative, their value dependent upon what came before, what came after, and the figures nearby. One hundred was a lot compared to ten, but not much compared to a thousand. Even with many additional zeros, the same held true.

"Don't worry," David said. "We already have way more than we need."

David had never spent much time thinking about money. When he was considering his original offer from Microsoft six years earlier and the president of the company called him, trying to convince him to join, he hadn't taken the opportunity to request a signing bonus. He didn't think to ask about more stock, either. Money hadn't been on his mind. He'd been trying to figure out if he liked the company and wasn't sure how he felt about moving across the country—and had ended up asking Microsoft's president for a few more days to think.

"My stock options make it easy to take a risk on Jeff's company," he said. "Do you realize my vested options are worth three million dollars?"

My stomach dropped.

"Three million dollars?" I said. "Is that all?"

After thinking we had ten million, with seven million dollars suddenly gone, and so many options being dangled in front of David, I wondered if my mother was right. Was I too interested in money? I'd never imagined craving bling or viewing three million dollars as nothing—but I did. Was money itself to blame? My reaction seemed so typical of the rich, evidence of greed.

But money wasn't corrupting me. Wealth hadn't clouded my thinking. I wasn't any more or less greedy than I'd been in the past. In fact, money wasn't changing me as much as I might have expected. It wasn't even changing me as much as I might have hoped. Like a truth serum, wealth seemed to be revealing more of who I was, exposing my desire for more sparkle and more options—and would eventually uncover my capacity for gratitude and generosity too.

Logically, and with some distance, I knew three million dollars was a fortune. But thinking about David leaving Microsoft, I wasn't considering the rest of the world or absolute sums. I was thinking about all the money he'd be leaving behind. I was also thinking about our coming baby, about the work required at a startup, and about our friends Donna, Matt, Lynn, and Adam who would still be at Microsoft, continuing to vest. I was thinking about David too, and wanted him to be happy. Following dreams was more important than financial reward. He could afford to take a risk. He loved the idea of playing with books and technology. He also wanted a new challenge. So, even though it was hard to let go of that much money, even as co-workers, friends, and Microsoft executives counseled him to stay, I encouraged David to follow his heart and take the Amazon job.

Contemplation & Conversation

- Jennifer's wish for a bigger diamond is driven, in part, by her desire to live up to the way the rich supposedly look and behave. Do you act or try to look as though you have more—or less—money than you actually do? Why?

- How did it make you feel to know Jennifer thought ten million dollars didn't sound like that much?

- Jennifer claims money hasn't changed her as much as she expected, or even as much as she might have hoped. Do you think wealth changes people or reveals who they are?

Chapter Five

MENTORS

In April 1997, with birds heralding our homecoming and azaleas in bloom, David and I pulled up to our house in Seattle, no longer the same two people we'd been forty-eight hours earlier. We were proud parents of a new baby girl.

David carried our daughter, Emily, up the front steps and into the house. Then, sitting on the sofa, we gazed in silence, mesmerized by the beautiful creature we'd brought into the world and right into our living room.

"Look at her nails," I said, holding her tiny hand, examining each finger. "Do they already need cutting?"

The miniature white moons were proof of a miracle. So was her small pink mouth and thick dark hair. But the intensity of my emotions was the biggest surprise. With Emily in the world, my heart had opened, turning me into the most vulnerable of beings and the strongest of women, empowered by feelings that were fierce and ferocious and humbled by the depth and immensity of love.

That night, I set my alarm.

"Will you set yours too?" I asked David. "Emily needs to eat every two hours. I want to make sure to wake up."

I fed Emily and nestled her into the cradle by our bed before sinking into my pillow, exhausted. Minutes later, at the sound of Emily's cry, I was upright in an instant. I nursed our daughter a second time, returned her to the cradle, and fell back into bed. But it wasn't long before I was awake again. After repeating the same routine several more times, I brought Emily into bed next to me, and was awake on and off—for seven months.

As my alarm became a thing of the past, days turned upside down. Showers happened after lunch and trips to the grocery store were three-hour expeditions. Emily's car seat became a new appendage, heavier and bulkier than it had appeared in the store or on other women's arms. Our stroller was twice as unwieldy too. I was also too tired to think. But even disorganized and fuzzyheaded, there was no way to go back. I didn't want to. It was as though a curtain had lifted and I'd entered a whole new world. Parents waved as I walked through the neighborhood. They greeted me with knowing smiles. Many fawned over Emily, admiring her beautiful smile, and making me feel united with every mother, father, and infant on earth.

Sitting at a coffee shop, Emily by my side, asleep in her stroller, I found it easy to meet other mothers. As soon as another woman wheeled up and sat down, we began talking about how much our babies weighed and how much they weren't sleeping. We spoke of the joys and difficulties of nursing, and shared the most intimate details of birth, equally surprised by the intensity of our own emotions.

Not only did I feel part of a whole new community, I felt closer to David. He too was in awe, thrilled to be a father. He gladly changed diapers, never complained about getting up in the middle of the night, and was proud of what he called the "daddy bounce." Standing on his tiptoes, knees bending, bopping up and down with Emily in his arms, he grinned at his ability to instill calm in his daughter. He also liked to strap on the BabyBjörn and go to the playground, jump on a swing, and fly into the air, Emily close to his chest. At the zoo, he pointed out the bears and the monkeys, teaching Emily what little he knew about animals. Growing up in Washington, D.C., seemingly far from farms and forests, he'd missed out on some of the basics, surprising me early on in our courtship when he mentioned he thought butter came from pigs.

In addition to bringing me closer to David, motherhood was something I shared with Donna and Lynn. Our daughters had been born within eight months of one another, and the three of us were going through a similar metamorphosis. No longer just women in the world, we were mothers with babies. But with Donna back at Microsoft and Lynn about to return, hoping to meet other new mothers, I signed up for a neighborhood mothers' group organized by a nonprofit called Program for Early Parenthood Support (PEPS).

For the first meeting, sixteen of us, all carrying babies and diaper bags, converged on the small brick home of our leader, who had rearranged her furniture to accommodate our group. A coffee table was in the entry hall, a sofa pushed against a wall, and several folding chairs were arranged in a semicircle in the living room. As we settled in, our leader, who was another relatively new mother and part of a PEPS group herself, explained that we would be getting together for the next twelve weeks, meeting every Monday in one another's homes to discuss the highs and lows of caring for an infant. She then asked us to introduce ourselves and our babies, and we went around the room, giving our names, briefly mentioning our work, then spending two hours telling birth stories.

We all lived within five miles of one another and were educated, capable, intelligent, middle- and upper middle-class women. We'd been pregnant, given birth, and the rhythm of our lives had changed. With all that in common, it didn't take long for a bond to form between us, our shared experience of becoming mothers giving us license and interest in diving deep into one another's lives and sharing our own. By the end of our second PEPS meeting, we were confiding in one another about our in-laws, divulging secrets about our sex lives, collectively rolling our eyes at all the baby weight we wanted to lose, and talking nonstop about sleep. None of us were getting enough, and we were equally interested in hearing strategies for how to get through the night without waking up every hour. We wanted to know the best methods for handling a crying baby too.

"If Ben is inconsolable, I put him in his car seat on the dryer," Carla said. "The sound and motion lull him to sleep."

"We go for a lot of long drives," Jill said.

After several weeks of meetings, we had united as a team. But when the conversation turned to baby gear, the differences in our economic situations, spending habits, and values began wedging their way between us. At first, we stuck to the facts, talking about stores we liked best and debating the usefulness of *Consumer Reports*. But as we discussed the specifics of strollers, cribs, and high chairs, with some women seizing on motherhood as an opportunity to shop and others limited to necessities, a divide began to grow.

"I just bought a Peg-Pérego stroller," Jill announced. "It's the best brand on the market."

"Those things are expensive!" Trish practically shouted.

"Yeah, I'm not spending three hundred dollars on a stroller," Grace said.

After six years cloistered within the homogeneous enclave of Microsoft millionaires, I'd unconsciously begun to assume everyone had stock options, which clearly wasn't the case. From outside my usual work routine, separate from the company, and getting to know a bunch of women who, like me, were new to motherhood, I was much more aware of how bizarre my life had become. Even by Microsoft standards, my circumstances were crazy.

Four months earlier, at the beginning of February 1997, after leaving Microsoft, David had spent a week cleaning our basement, doing his own form of nesting before heading downtown to work at "Earth's Biggest Bookstore." During the months that followed, he'd begun helping Amazon create "Earth's Biggest Selection," adding music, videos, and toys to the company's product line. Then, in May 1997, four weeks after Emily's birth, Amazon had gone public, and in one day, David's share in the company had become worth forty million dollars.

Forty million dollars! The amount was obscene. It was more than my head could comprehend. Yes, I was amazed. But all that money made me uneasy. I didn't know what it would mean for my life. Did I need to make changes? Would people look at me differently? I'd heard the rich worried about being liked only for their money, never sure which friendships were authentic and which were financially based. But I wasn't concerned about people liking me for my money. I was worried they'd hate me for it—and didn't want anyone to know.

As other mothers in our PEPS group continued talking about the price of strollers, I was silent. I stayed quiet when everyone shared stories about how hard it was to comfort their babies in the evening too. It didn't seem wise to share my frustration at David's long hours. If anyone thought too much about his job, they might guess at our situation and resent my complaining. Or maybe they'd wonder how I could possibly be struggling. Wasn't money supposed to make all problems disappear?

Back before Microsoft, Amazon, and Emily, if anyone had asked if a million dollars could bring happiness, my spontaneous, frivolous response would have been, "Of course!" Then, with a minute to think, I'd have righteously proclaimed, "Money can't buy happiness. Contentment and joy have to come from within and can't be purchased." But thinking for a few more minutes, looking deeper, I'd have imagined a million dollars getting me closer, easing me nearer, setting me in the direction toward contentment. How could it not? Several layers into the question, with actual experience, I was discovering the connection between money and happiness was even more enigmatic that I'd once thought. Some days, it seemed money was only changing my life for the better. We had a nice house, two cars, and the ability to travel. Our future looked bright. Other days, stock options hadn't changed a thing. I was still the same person. My feelings got hurt. I worried too much. I was fearful of not fitting in, always trying to prove my worth. Amazon stock wasn't keeping me from being exhausted or stopping me from craving friendship and connection. My desires, needs, and anxieties remained. I hadn't changed, not down deep where it counted. More than that, wealth seemed to be adding to my stress, creating new dilemmas and worries. I was part of a great group of women but didn't feel comfortable sharing what was really going on in my life. I couldn't imagine admitting to having so much money, let alone complaining about being uncomfortable and embarrassed. I couldn't imagine admitting to being anything less than perfectly happy. I didn't want to sound ungrateful. I didn't want to be judged.

Over the years that followed, it would be hard not to hear disdain in comments like "What problems do you have?" or "Must be nice." It was painful to be dismissed. I didn't like hearing people use wealth as an explanation for obnoxious behavior either. Once, over lunch, I listened in silence as a friend talked about how stressful it was to work with rich clients.

"They're so demanding," she said.

Seemingly unaware of her own bias, or of hurting my feelings, she continued to bemoan the challenge of dealing with people who had a lot of money. But did irritating behavior truly have its roots in money? Wasn't it unfair to stereotype people? Why did no one at the table object to her remarks? Instead, most nodded. Prejudice against the rich not only seemed acceptable, it was condoned, practically applauded.

At the time, maybe I should have spoken up, but I didn't want to create conflict. Years later, when I finally started talking about wealth with friends whose circumstances were like my own, I found comfort in knowing I wasn't alone. One friend, who had married into a wealthy family, told me she too was frustrated when people responded to her wealth and not to her as a person. When she wanted to get back into tennis and asked a woman who played how to get started, the woman looked at her, paused, and said, "You'll want to play at The Pines," a nearby country club.

"She didn't tell me about the tennis community at the public park or invite me to join her team," my friend said. "I didn't get the same information she would have given someone else."

Another friend, Denise, whose husband had sold his technology company for an extreme amount of money, told me how upsetting it was to have people come to their home and comment on her perfect, problem-free life.

"Normally, I understand. People think living in a nice house makes everything perfect. But when things weren't going well between my husband and me, and a houseguest said how easy my life must be living where we live, I had a hard time just smiling and staying quiet. Maybe I should have said something. They didn't mean to upset me."

At the time, my closest friends in the PEPS group were Carla and Grace, and neither was buying designer strollers. Carla and I had shared a sense of wonder the first day our group met, both of us enthralled by our babies as they lay side by side on blankets in front of us. We later discovered a mutual love of cooking and had begun to share recipes and dinner ideas. Grace and I also got along well. During our first meeting, Grace captured everyone's attention when she told the group she had a three-year-old at home. None of us could imagine caring for a toddler as well as an infant, and it was impressive to see how well she handled the job. She was fun to be around, often showing up Monday morning sporting a new hairstyle and telling us about creating life-sized sculptures of her nude upper torso, the latest of which she had covered with tiny seashells and was painting gold.

While Carla and Grace were becoming my friends, two other women in the group had caught my attention as well. In the past, I would have labeled and dismissed them: one flashy and bold, the other distant and aloof. But even as I dubbed them Ms. Glamor and Ms. Old Money, I wanted to understand who they were and how they handled their wealth.

At our first meeting, Ms. Glamor had slouched on the sofa under a blanket, saying she was completely overwhelmed. Just a few weeks later, not only had she pulled herself together, she began to sparkle and shine. Like a socialite pretending to be a movie star, she waltzed into Monday morning, shrugged off her Armani raincoat, sat down with a flash of her three-carat diamond, and made flamboyant statements.

"I gained so much weight during pregnancy," she said. "I had to buy a whole new wardrobe of disposable clothes at Mervyn's."

She announced her plan to replace the Alfa Romeo she'd been driving with a bigger, safer car. She was on the lookout for a bigger house too.

"But prices are so outrageous these days," she bemoaned. "You can't find a teardown for less than a million."

She then turned up the volume.

"How much is enough? What's your number?" she asked,

looking around the room. "My husband says he'd be satisfied with thirty million dollars."

Most of the other women seemed to brush off the comment or laugh at the idea, but I sat forward in my chair. This tall, attractive woman with platinum blonde hair and pouty red lips may have been throwing around astronomical numbers and snubbing stores where other women shopped, but she had so much confidence and bravado. She had no shame around wealth.

One Monday morning, Ms. Glamor showed up in a low-cut, leopard-print cashmere sweater, oversized pearls, and black stovepipe pants.

"I wouldn't have the guts to wear an outfit like that," I told her.

"You could pull it off," she said, looking askance at my comfortable jeans. "It's all about attitude. Who cares what people think?"

Another morning, Ms. Glamor held her daughter in the air, showing us the Baby Dior dress she'd found at a children's designer boutique having a sale. As she raved about the cute Italian and French fashions, waves of contention and admiration rippled through the room. Grace whispered something about how quickly baby clothes get outgrown. Carla muttered how ridiculous it was to spend so much on a baby. Trish said she wished she could afford the same dress for her daughter.

"Where exactly is the store?" someone asked.

I wanted to know about the store too, but I didn't say anything. I didn't want anyone to suspect we had money, and felt guilty about my interest in shopping.

When I started elementary school, my mother took up sewing. The two of us enjoyed picking out patterns and looking at material for the skirts and tops she made for me. But when I hit junior high and was more fashion conscious, and more self-conscious too, I no longer wanted clothes made by my mom, and begged her for the jeans other kids were wearing.

"Everyone has 501s," I said. "I really want a pair."

"You already have jeans," she said.

"But those aren't the same."

My mother didn't understand my interest in Sbicca rope shoes, a satin jacket, or the right look either.

"Spend more time reading and less time worrying about your appearance," she told me.

"You don't get it," I yelled.

After years of arguing about clothes with my mother, it was hard for me to admit my interest in looking at dresses for Emily. But lured by thoughts of beautiful European styling at a discount, I asked Ms. Glamor about the store in private. Unconsciously, I hoped she might sanction my spending. Maybe she would sanction my wealth. Perhaps she'd see me as an equal, even a friend. But when she suggested we go shopping together, I panicked. She was so glamorous. How would I ever keep up? She might discover the extent of my cluelessness and that I wasn't good at spending. But I agreed to meet her at the store.

"I almost bought this sweater last time I was here," she said, holding up a small white cardigan with yellow ducklings circling the collar. "Isn't it adorable?"

We wandered through the boutique, admiring the miniature clothing hanging on tiny hangers and folded on shelves.

"Look at this!" Ms. Glamor said, holding up a tiny, blue frilly dress with matching bloomers. "Do you think it's my daughter's color?

It was fun to lose myself in silk embroidery, browsing through cotton pants, floppy hats, and little tailored jackets. With Ms. Glamor by my side, I gave myself permission to buy several outfits. Spending money on Emily was a lot easier than spending on myself.

After saying good-bye to Ms. Glamor and driving home, I thought back to when she had told our PEPS group how much she and her husband loved to shop.

"Shopping is my forte," she'd said. "It's what my husband and I do best."

At the time, her pronouncement had been bewildering. Why would anyone brag about something so superficial? But after joining Ms. Glamor at the boutique, searching through stacks of cotton onesies and rows of cute dresses, I understood she was just having fun. I'd had fun too. An interest in clothes didn't make her a bad person. The way she spent money didn't determine her worth. Saving didn't make me responsible either. I may have been using Ms. Glamor to justify my purchases, but suddenly, I realized that the way a person handles money doesn't dictate their value. It was a revelation!

Not long after Ms. Glamor and I went shopping together, she announced to our PEPS group that she was looking for a part-time job. Soon afterward, pursuing her passion for retail, using her style and good taste, she landed a position as a saleswoman at a children's boutique.

"It's great to earn my own pocket money," she told us.

As Ms. Glamor helped me disentangle my beliefs about saving, spending, and being responsible, I benefited from a friendship with Ms. Old Money as well. At first, she seemed easy to peg, showing up to our PEPS meetings in conservative sweater sets and squeaky-clean tennis whites, looking as though she'd stepped out of *The Official Preppy Handbook* from the 1980s. She made sure everyone knew her parents were affiliated with the most prestigious organizations throughout the city, that her college sorority was full of women from good families, and that she was a longtime member of the Seattle Tennis Club. Gravitating toward the women in our group who appeared to share her socioeconomic standing, she practically ignored those who didn't reach her bar, often scanning the room and handing down judgments, thinking of herself as better than the rest of us.

"Do you remember when I left our first meeting early?" she asked me one morning. "I wanted to check out another group, to see if there were more women like me."

Although her comment made me cringe, interested in understanding what was behind her buttoned-up, Lilly Pulitzer exterior, I joined her at the park, the two of us sitting in the sun with our daughters in strollers by our sides. And as we got to know one another, I realized Ms. Old Money didn't feel as superior as her appearance and attitude implied—or as I'd believed. She'd grown up with an alcoholic father, lost her younger brother to an accident in high school, and was looking for understanding and companionship. When she told me how much she loved spending afternoons at the Seattle Tennis Club, playing tennis and sitting by the pool, she was sharing what was going on in her life. She wasn't bragging or showing off. Her club may have been exclusive, but just as our PEPS group helped both of us find common ground in motherhood, her club gave her a place to belong where she could connect with people whose circumstances were like her own and speak freely without fear of being judged—by people like me.

Meanwhile, I got yet another perspective on wealth from a woman who worked at Amazon with David.

"I joined a mothers' group too," she told me. "At first, the common experience of motherhood was the bond. Everyone's baby cries and spits up. But it felt odd. I had this incredible fortune at Amazon and was caught between wanting to share my excitement and not wanting to alienate people. When my son was eight months old, I was invited to speak at a conference in Sydney but didn't want to leave our son. It was frustrating not to be able to share the details of my dilemma with the group. It didn't feel appropriate to discuss paying to bring my mother and son with me. Since I wanted to talk about what was going on in my life, I joined a different group. In the new group, the question wasn't whether to get a nanny, it was whether to hire a night nurse and a cook too. We discussed kid-friendly hotels and houses to rent in Europe. It was the kind of information that was relevant to my changing life. It was what I wanted and needed."

I understood the desire to enjoy life without worrying about alienating others, but I liked my PEPS group. Then, one day, Carla told me Trish hated hosting us at her house.

"When it's her turn to have us over, she's afraid people feel they have to slum it," Carla said. "Before our group started getting together, she thought she was doing fine. Now, being around everyone else, she feels poor. I think she's going to stop coming to our meetings."

"Really? I had no idea," I said. "No one cares how much money she has."

"Maybe you don't," Carla said. "But she feels self-conscious and can't relax when we get together. To be honest, I feel it too. Other people have told me they have a hard time being around Ms. Glamor . . . and you."

I was stunned, my feelings hurt. Did people know about my situation? Had I been making others uncomfortable? While I'd been looking to Ms. Glamor and Ms. Old Money as role models, had other women been watching—and judging—me?

I never asked these questions out loud. It made me uncomfortable to even consider talking about money. While my changing circumstances had compelled me to get to know Ms. Glamor and Ms. Old Money, none of the other women needed to examine their assumptions or put up with people who made them uneasy.

Contemplation & Conversation

- Do you try to keep your financial situation hidden? Do you think your relationships would change if people knew how much money you had?

- How does money connect or disconnect you from other people?

Chapter Six

MORE THAN A PAYCHECK

For years, I imagined the glory and wonder of not having to work. I pictured freedom and choices, sunny days, walks on beaches, long lunches, and friends. I'd get up in the morning, the day stretched before me, glowing with opportunity and anticipation, mine to shape and fill in any way I liked. I hadn't anticipated not knowing what to do with my time. I hadn't appreciated the goals and structure a job gave me either. Nor had I contemplated the struggle to define myself as others looked longingly in my direction.

When my maternity leave ended, I left Microsoft to be with Emily. I wanted to be with our daughter, and there was no financial reason to return to my job. In many ways, the decision was obvious. But as the Microsoft doors closed behind me for good, I began to realize my identity was caught up in work.

Work had always been an important part of my life. I'd wanted to be like my father, rushing out the door in the morning with business to accomplish, returning in the evening, admired and respected. During high school, I'd worked at a roadside fruit stand, sorting produce and serving customers. Summers during college, I filled in for the receptionist, the mail guy, and various secretaries at an insurance agency in Portland, happy to be helping. Then, after graduating from college, I taught English in Tokyo for two years, experiencing a new culture before moving to Seattle and working my way into that advertising agency. At Microsoft, as a recruiter and a member of a product group, I loved being on a team, connected and involved, solving problems and getting things done. When people asked, "What do you do?" I answered with pride.

In the 1990s, when I left Microsoft, women were supposedly breaking through the glass ceiling, able to have it all. But it wasn't easy to be a mother with a career. Fathers rarely took a fifty-fifty role in childcare or household management, and the long hours required to succeed within a high-powered workplace were not compatible with pregnancy, childbirth, maternity leave, and a baby. To make the situation worse, mothers like Lynn, Donna, and me, who had the luxury of choice, competed with one another. Perhaps we were all trying to justify our decisions, but mothers who worked looked down on those who stayed home and vice versa, each making snide comments like, "I simply *need* to use my brain," or "I can't *imagine* leaving my child."

When her maternity leave ended, Lynn was thrilled to return to the recruiting department at Microsoft. She craved the stimulation of being in an office and wanted to keep her skills up to date. Bringing home a paycheck gave her satisfaction as well. Donna was working too. But unlike Lynn, who was content with her position, Donna wanted to advance and was frustrated by her inability to work at the same pace and level as before her daughter was born. Although Microsoft policies were family-friendly, most employees were single, male, and eager to spend eighty hours in the office every week. Even in HR, the one department where women were in the majority, men dominated the culture. Or, at least, the culture was dominated by employees who didn't have children. No one left early or came in late. Managers did not display photos of babies on their desks or talk about being parents.

"I'm not doing anything well," Donna told me. "I'm not a good mom or a good employee, and it's annoying that nothing has changed for Matt."

Even though Donna's job was as meaningful to her as Matt's was to him, whether by choice, default, or the power of cultural norms and gender roles, Donna was the one scrambling to get to the daycare by six o'clock. She was also planning the evening meals, buying groceries, and doing the cooking.

"My life is being held together by a rubber band," she said. "One wrong move and 'snap!'"

I empathized with Donna and was thankful to be at home with Emily. Conventional wisdom of the time dictated that children were better off with a parent at home, and as a rule follower, I was glad to be doing the "right" thing. It was fun to take Emily to music class and Gymboree. What's more, with no impending workweek, I experienced Sunday evenings in a whole new, stress-free way. Weekday mornings were more relaxed too. But I missed my job. When the alarm on David's side of the bed went off and he headed to the office, driven by the excitement of adding new offerings to Amazon's product line, I felt left behind. It also bothered me not to be contributing to our family financially. I wasn't bringing home a paycheck.

I'd cashed in my options. Even though the cost of a household manager, nanny, and cook gave my presence at home monetary value, being a wife and mother made me feel like a second-class citizen.

Our growing wealth only added to my angst. Given David's continued success, we were often invited to exclusive, business-related or fundraising events where I found myself standing with a cocktail in my hand, chatting with overachievers, dreading the question, "What do you do?" It could be an honest attempt to get acquainted and find common ground, but this question made me nervous. What did I do? Who was I anyway? Was it enough to just be a mother at home? Should I return to work? What was my purpose? Did I have any value?

As a mom at home, I was on a path most people in business didn't understand or respect. Hearing, usually from a man who would never consider leaving work, that caring for children was the most important job a person could do, I felt as though I was getting a pat on the head, not the back. I hated imagining people looking at me as a high net worth individual or worse, as the wife of a rich husband. At one fundraising dinner, seated next to Howard Schultz, then CEO of Starbucks, I considered talking about rationing my lattes, but ended up making small talk, feeling like someone who had slipped in as ". . . and guest."

Decades later, my brother would say he thought our wealth robbed me of the opportunity to prove myself. Without a job, I didn't get the chance to feel successful. In many ways, he was right. I missed out on a career. For years, I longed for the sense of accomplishment in achieving business goals and missed the camaraderie of being part of a team, doing what people do, working together, involved in something bigger than myself. At the same time, I'd made the choice to be home with our daughter, and I would make it again.

Looking for a sense of purpose and a way to connect with other new mothers, I explored volunteer options. When I discovered a nonprofit that worked with pregnant teens, I signed up to be a mentor. After going through a brief training program, I was paired with Keiko, an eighteen-year-old from Japan who had come to the United States as a student, gotten pregnant, and was planning to stay. When we first got together, I trotted out one of the few Japanese phrases I remembered from my time in Tokyo, "A train is approaching. Please stand behind the yellow line. It's dangerous to get too close." Hearing this, Keiko laughed, and a connection formed between us.

During the weeks that followed, I drove Keiko to the hospital for checkups and showed her how to get vouchers for formula. We spent time at the park, playing with Emily and talking about pregnancy. Highly aware of the disparity between us, I wanted to take her out for lunch, offer her cash, and buy clothes and toys for her coming baby, but the nonprofit that brought us together didn't allow volunteers to give financial assistance.

When the programmed three months of our time together ended, Keiko and I had each benefited from knowing the other. But we lost touch when she moved to Los Angeles with her boyfriend. Soon after, I signed up to become a leader of a PEPS group like my own, and again went through a training course to learn about facilitating discussions and ensuring everyone felt heard.

"It's too bad we can't bring our babies with us when we lead a group," a fellow trainee said to me the last day. "I'll have to wait until the summer when my mom can watch my son."

"It's nice your mom is nearby," I said. "I don't know what I'll do. It's hard to imagine leaving my daughter with a stranger. Do you know any good daycares?"

"What? Daycare? But you aren't working," she said. "How can you justify paying for daycare?"

She looked at me in disbelief.

"How can you afford it?" she continued. "Are you really going to pay someone else so you can work for free?"

Her astonishment was understandable. So was her exasperation. She was clearly irritated to imagine me paying someone to watch Emily. Wasn't I supposed to have just learned to empathize with others? Did I completely lack discretion? Was I always going to make other people uncomfortable? Embarrassed, I mumbled something about being lucky and rushed out the door.

Unlike Donna and Lynn, who had socially acceptable reasons to put their daughters in daycare, I wasn't working and didn't *need* to leave Emily with strangers. Was I being selfish, shirking my responsibility? Would Emily be okay? Unsure of the answer, but eager to lead a PEPS group, I toured a few daycares. And when I discovered a place with wonderful caregivers, I signed Emily up for two mornings a week and joined the daycare's board, looking forward to getting involved.

Leading a mothers' group was rewarding. My presence was a benefit to eighteen new moms and their babies. Every week, I facilitated discussions and made sure everyone felt heard and included. But over time, rather than becoming part of the growing companionship that was forming among the women in the group, since leaders weren't supposed to talk about their own experiences, I found myself on the outside again.

One day, a friend asked me to join her for a tour of Pike Place Market, Seattle's historic marketplace near the waterfront. Tim Kelley, a young chef from The Painted Table, a highly regarded restaurant, led our group through the market's produce stalls and showed us how to choose the freshest ingredients. He then took us to The Painted Table for a cooking demonstration and lunch. As I stood in the restaurant's kitchen, watching Tim seed, chop, and squeeze tomatoes through cheesecloth to extract "tomato water," I wanted to get to work. I'd always loved cooking and was intrigued by the restaurant business. It looked fun to be part of the kitchen team. Once the demonstration was over and lunch had been served, I summoned my courage and asked Tim if he could use a helper for a day, thrilled when he agreed to let me work for free.

A few weeks later, after dropping Emily at daycare, I drove directly to The Painted Table where Tim gave me a brief tour of the kitchen, handed me five blackened red peppers, showed me how to remove the char, and left me alone to complete the task. When Tim returned half an hour later, he thanked me and gave me another assignment chopping several pounds of mushrooms.

I was focused on my job when the lunch staff arrived. Soon, the first order swung through the door in the form of a waiter who clipped a white paper to a rotating steel ring, turned, and disappeared. As more orders followed, a circus began. The team juggled fire, whipped sauces, and threw burning pans into the sink. Jokes were cracked, demands shouted, and obscenities flew. Three hours passed in an instant. Then, just as quickly as it reached a rolling boil, the kitchen was back to a slow simmer, and Tim suggested I make myself lunch.

"Cook anything you want," he said before disappearing out the swinging door.

Alone in the kitchen, I stepped up to the stove, planning to copy the wilted spinach salad Debbie, the lunchtime sous chef, had prepared with the mushrooms I'd chopped. When my dish was ready, I ate standing up, hungry for more. A four-hour stint wasn't nearly long enough. So, I tracked Tim down, thanked him profusely, and asked if I could return every Friday. He agreed.

Over several months of Fridays, my de-charring and chopping skills improved, and I graduated to preparing the pasta to order. Grabbing for olive oil, minced garlic, and julienned vegetables, I jumped into the lunchtime fire, thrilled to be creating a dish that would be served to a customer in the dining room. Deploying my new skills and losing myself in my work, I was reminded of Joseph Conrad's quote from *Heart of Darkness*: "I like what is in the work—the chance to find yourself. Your own reality—for yourself not for others—what no other man can ever know. They can only see the mere show, and never can tell what it really means."

Debbie appeared proud of her job. In her late twenties, with jet-black hair and a pierced upper lip, she was confident and tough. It wasn't easy to be a woman in a professional kitchen, and she'd proven herself by moving up the ranks. She clearly had a passion and talent for her work. Searing a hunk of fish in oil, sliding the pan into the oven, then sensing when it was done, she removed the fillet from the heat, placed it artfully on a bed of crushed fingerling potatoes, added herbs and a drizzle of oil, and yelled for a waiter. She wanted her dish served hot.

Rob, the guy at the grill, seemed to enjoy his work. He showed up promptly at eleven o'clock to churn out tasty-looking plates with efficiency and focus. He was also generous with smiles and advice, often sharing recipes and telling me anecdotes about life as a chef. When lunch was over and dinner was prepped, he headed out the door.

"I love doing this. It's stress-free," he told me. "I've been head chef in other places, but it's more fun to work the grill. I get to hang out. I get paid. And I don't have any responsibility."

Meanwhile, Tim, a rising star, was king of the kitchen. With a quick wit and dynamic personality, he seemed driven to succeed, sweeping into the lunchtime scene issuing commands and demanding excellence. But he wasn't satisfied. Several times, he asked me if he should invest in Microsoft and Amazon, and in the months to come, seemingly in search of further fame and fortune, he would move to New York City.

One morning, Rob asked why I was spending so much time in the kitchen. Afraid he had me pegged as an overly privileged housewife with too much time on her hands, I wasn't sure what to say. The label fit. It was valid. But I was too uncomfortable with the truth to talk about my situation. Instead, I shrugged, saying I was lucky to have extra time. There was no way I could admit to being a rich woman, playing around at making lunch.

Looking back, I imagine my evasive non-answer was annoying. Rob wasn't oblivious. It was probably irritating to hear me avoid the facts he'd likely surmised. I should have told him I was having fun in the kitchen, excited to be learning new skills, getting to know the team, and thankful for the stories and advice he'd shared. I should have acknowledged our crazy fortune too. I could have let him know it was strange. I could have shared more about my life with the PEPS group I was leading and been more authentic with the woman at the training session too. If I'd told her I was fortunate but found my situation odd and lonely, I might have come across as clueless and awkward, but at least I would have shown up and given her an opportunity to respond. Similarly, if I'd joked with Howard Schultz about rationing my lattes while working in advertising or talked about the transition from workplace to home, dinner conversation would have been a lot more enjoyable. As it was, it would take years to get comfortable as a stay-at-home mother and wealthy woman. I didn't *feel* like either. It would also take years not to dread the question, "What do you do?"

Contemplation & Conversation

- Jennifer identified with her job and had a hard time feeling her value outside of the workforce. Do you identify with your work? In addition to a paycheck, what else do you get out of your job? If you're not working, how do you define yourself?

- What is your experience with work and parenthood? Has one taken precedence over another? What role has money played in your decisions? How have you and your partner negotiated work, parenthood, and money?

Chapter Seven

LUXURY

Months after getting engaged, with the help of James, David and I found and purchased a 1915 Colonial on a tree-lined street, thrilled to have a place of our own. At $312,000, the house was much nicer than a fixer-upper and bigger than the houses either of us lived in growing up. With three stories and in a nice neighborhood, it was also way beyond what most couples in their early thirties could afford. But we simply cashed in stock options. And with co-workers and friends living in similarly sized and even grander places, I saw our house as normal.

My view of travel was similarly warped. After taking a trip to Greece, David and I had vacationed in Morocco. We'd then gone to Portugal and Spain for our honeymoon. So, when we talked about where to go next, Hawaii sounded boring. Where was the fun and sense of adventure in staying so close to home? We wouldn't be learning to say "thank you" in a foreign language or experiencing a different culture. I didn't like the idea of just sitting around doing nothing. On the other hand, Hawaii was family-friendly and with Emily just eight months old, we decided to go.

Arriving at the Kea Lani in Wailea, we were greeted by smiling women in long, flowing dresses who placed purple leis around our necks and tropical juice in our hands. We then wandered the open-air lobby and let Emily splash her feet in the fountain until a man in a blue and white flowered shirt introduced himself as Gary and offered to show us to our suite. After changing into swimsuits and taking a few photos of Emily looking cute in her bikini, we headed outside.

Half-naked toddlers were running across the freshly cut lawn and rows of adults in colorful swimwear were sitting at the swim-up bar. In the water, groups of children were tossing beach balls and screaming "Marco Polo." Looking forward to showing Emily the wonder of sand and the thrill of the ocean, we walked past the pool toward the beach, where David began crawling around, coaxing Emily to follow. He dug holes and suggested sand castles. But Emily didn't want to leave the comfort of the terrycloth. She didn't even want her feet to touch the ground. And when David picked her up and we walked toward the ocean, she burst into tears.

Back at the pool, it was obvious that baby-blue tiles and sparkling clear water were more welcoming than loud surf and hot sand. Emily clapped with excitement and tossed herself into the water. David caught her, put her back on the side of the pool, and she launched herself into the water again, giving us our first glimpse of the repetition she would continue to love. When it came to *Brown Bear, Brown Bear* and *Goodnight Moon*, and then to the movies *101 Dalmatians* and *A Bug's Life*, Emily wanted to hear the same words and see the same pictures over and over again. She was learning about herself and her world.

During our time in Maui, David and I also enjoyed repetition, waking with the sun every morning, relaxing over breakfast, then jumping, splashing, and playing at the pool until naptime. Every evening, when the tiki guy made his rounds, lighting torches to inaugurate the cocktail hour, we made our biggest decision of the day—where to go for dinner. With time and familiarity, we were learning about our world too, and I was becoming increasingly comfortable with doing nothing but relaxing. In fact, enjoying the wonders of Hawaii, ten days on Maui became something I wanted to repeat—every year.

In the middle of the night, however, my eyes popped open, my thoughts glued to Emily. Were we setting her up to be spoiled? If she only experienced Hawaiian vacations and exotic travel and never had to make trade-offs or stay at home, would she become entitled? Was all this luxury harming our daughter? For hours, I was unable to sleep.

The next morning, in the light and warmth of the Hawaiian sun, the monstrous question of whether our vacation was spoiling our daughter didn't loom quite as large—until we were perusing the breakfast buffet, choosing from guava and papaya, homemade pastries and breads, sausage and bacon, pancakes, waffles, and eggs made to order.

"Do you think Emily is becoming spoiled?" I asked David.

"She's eight months old," he replied. "She's just living life."

As a Microsoft employee, I knew my medical benefits were good, but didn't understand how truly excellent they were. Except for employees who wore glasses and raved about the free pair they could get every year, no one at Microsoft talked about healthcare. Most everyone was too young and too healthy to need or to use insurance and none of my friends or acquaintances were suffering from illness or injury. Healthcare wasn't yet a topic of discussion in our country either. So, while I knew, intellectually, that medical coverage was a benefit, I didn't think of healthcare as a luxury. It shouldn't be.

When my period never resumed after Emily's birth, I didn't think twice about the cost of seeing a doctor. Nor was I worried about the price of the hormones she recommended, or about returning for a second appointment when the medicine she'd prescribed didn't kick my system into action. When my blood-work came back normal, I wasn't concerned about seeing an endocrinologist. I simply got the care I needed, which included an MRI. When the results came back normal and there still were no answers to why my period hadn't resumed, I made an appointment at a fertility clinic, where David and I sat together in a small, sterile room, waiting for yet another doctor's diagnosis.

"The ultrasound indicates no activity in the ovaries," the doctor said.

"What does that mean?" David asked.

"No eggs are being produced. There's no way to get pregnant if eggs aren't being released. Clomid can often jumpstart ovulation. In your case, it will take something stronger."

As the doctor continued, explaining that injections would be necessary, that there was a fifty-fifty chance of conception, and multiples were likely, it was hard for me to digest the information. In a matter-of-fact way, he stated that the cost of treatment was thousands of dollars, and while David signed us up for a class on how to use a needle, I walked out of the room and down the street to the car. The doctor's nonchalance was upsetting. More than that, I was scared of not being able to get pregnant again. Would we have another baby? Would Emily be a big sister?

David caught up to me at the car.

"No way!" I said. "I'm not taking those drugs."

"It's not a big deal," he said. "People do it all the time."

"Maybe it's not a big deal for you."

"Fertility drugs can be highly successful," he said.

"Highly successful? What are you talking about? What does that even mean?"

David's voice grew calm as he reminded me of the statistics.

"You sound like the doctor," I yelled.

"You're being irrational," David countered.

"This is a big deal. I may never get pregnant," I hissed.

"Oh. I see. *You* may never get pregnant," he bit back. "Well, if *we* want another baby, this is *our* best option."

"Don't be patronizing. And stop talking about options. It's like this hasn't affected you at all."

"Oh, that's nice," David said.

By the time we pulled up to the house, neither of us was speaking.

Rocking with Emily, staring out the window past the yellow curtains at the trees, I knew my infertility was not only a physical problem. I wasn't just a body. My mental, emotional, and spiritual states were impacting my ability to get pregnant as well. So, to find answers, I took a holistic approach. I tried homeopathic remedies, acupuncture, and hypnotherapy. Without giving much thought to the fact that most people couldn't afford to explore and experiment, I made an appointment with a therapist as well.

My first session was humbling. Overwhelmed by a rush of messy emotions, I wanted to run, never to return. All those chaotic feelings didn't belong to me! I didn't *need* to see a therapist. But with a deep sadness welling up from within, I broke down in tears. Not only did I stay in my seat, I agreed to return the following week.

Newly aware of my own anxiety, I started a process that would prove to be one of the most difficult, meaningful, and satisfying endeavors of my life. For five years, being as open and honest with myself as possible, I talked about my childhood. I also learned to see myself more clearly and find self-acceptance. Slowly, I built confidence too. Only looking back did I realize my therapist and I never talked about money. The wealth David and I had was growing. My identity was challenged and I didn't know where I fit into the world. And yet, money was a topic my therapist and I never discussed. In part, I avoided it. But my therapist avoided it too. Money was a taboo subject.

Many years later, reading a book called *The New Elite* by Dr. Jim Taylor, Doug Harrison, and Stephen Kraus, I was relieved to learn many newly wealthy people grapple with identity and sense of place. Based on interviews, focus groups, and quantitative surveys with over 6,000 wealthy participants, *The New Elite* reported it could often take years—even decades—for people to shed their upbringing and get comfortable with wealth. Intellectually, people knew their status had changed but emotionally it took time for them to *feel* wealthy.

"It is almost as if their self-concepts are frozen in their middle-class upbringings, largely untouched by the metamorphosis of their financial situation," the authors wrote.

"When a person experiences sudden wealth, there's more fallout and readjustment than you ever would have dreamed of," said Moira Somers, a neuropsychologist based in Winnipeg, Canada who works with the wealthy. Moira likened the experience of sudden wealth to mentioning your love of beef to a friend, then having two thousand head of cattle arrive as a gift to your door.

"What the hell do you do with two thousand steer?" she said. "You need to know how to deal with them and that's very different than eating a steak."

Six months after I began searching for answers to why my period hadn't returned, I was glad David had negotiated vacation time when he started at Amazon, and thankful we could afford to take another great one. This time, David, Emily, and I spent two weeks in Spain.

As David checked us into the Marbella Club, a five-star spa and resort in the south of Spain, I followed Emily as she toddled a few laps around the lobby. A gentleman in a suit then gathered up our bags and chauffeured us in a golf cart to our suite by the sea. For a week, we did nothing but relax, playing in the pool and strolling along the beach. But on the night before our departure, while David and Emily were dreaming, I was awake once again, staring at the canopy over the four-poster bed, wondering how we would keep Emily from becoming spoiled. She'd just spent a week being served breakfast on the terrace by the pool. When I was her age, our family wasn't travelling internationally. We weren't travelling at all. My mother was saving the second half of my breakfast banana to have the next day.

Taking a deep breath and looking around the dark room, conscious of the fine fabrics and beautifully hand-painted tiles, aware of David in bed next to me and our sweet daughter asleep nearby, I felt the abundance in my life. I was lucky. But I also knew what was important. It was dangerously easy to lose track of our advantages, but I didn't need to fret myself into a future that didn't exist. Emily wasn't a spoiled brat just because she wasn't growing up the way I had. Nor was she doomed to becoming entitled—not if I remained aware and respectful of the people around me and appreciative of all the luxuries in our life. An exotic vacation at a high-end resort was a wonderful benefit. So was being able to spend the day at the beach. But vacationing in Spain would not have been the same without Emily and David. Being with the people I loved was what mattered most.

The next morning, I was grateful for a long, hot shower and enjoyed pancakes and eggs with David and Emily. Back in Seattle, my sense of abundance grew. I hadn't viewed pregnancy as a luxury before, but after struggling with infertility, more aware of how fortunate we were to have Emily, I felt an even greater sense of amazement. There had been no drugs or injections. My period still hadn't resumed. And yet, our second child was on the way. I was pregnant again!

"It's the work I'm doing in therapy," I told David. "Getting to know and accept myself, I'm more relaxed."

"Or maybe it was the vacation we just took," he said.

It was true. Many factors contributed to my ability to get pregnant: a European vacation, excellent healthcare, and a comfortable home. Awareness and appreciation of life's abundance played a role too.

With a second baby on the way, David and I felt the need for a more family-friendly car. But when we walked into the Volvo dealership, rather than embracing the luxury of being able to afford one, I was on edge. Fearful of some slick salesmen taking advantage of us, when a young man in a suit sauntered over to offer his help, I shook my head and turned away.

"Actually," David said. "We'd like to test drive the new S80."

For half an hour, we drove around the neighborhood, the salesman talking nonstop about the car's smooth ride and safety record which, to me, only proved the stereotype. Back at the dealership, as we sat down at the salesman's desk, David seemed prepared to continue listening patiently. But I didn't want to be manipulated.

"We just want the car," I said, cutting the salesman off.

"There are several special packages included on this vehicle," he said. "I'd like to tell you about them."

"I'm not interested. I just want the car," I said again.

But the salesman continued talking.

"What's your best price?" I demanded, standing up.

David touched my arm, suggesting I get some fresh air while he finished the transaction, but I continued my rant, wielding our wealth like a sword.

"We're paying in cash," I said, storming around the dealership, pulling out my checkbook. "I'm ready to write a check, right here, right now."

Looking back, I'd like to blame my unpleasant behavior on pregnancy. Hormones were raging. But anxiety had me advancing an ugly stereotype of my own. Using wealth to try to get what I wanted and avoid what I didn't, I showed no regard for the salesman or anyone else in the dealership. I'd lost track of life's abundance and exhibited the kind of behavior I never wanted to repeat and certainly didn't want to see from Emily.

Luckily, my reaction was more balanced and aware several months later when David told me he'd purchased a BMW 3 Series on a whim, without me.

"Come outside and have a look," he said, eager to show me his new toy. "My Toyota was having problems. It was time."

Years earlier, I wouldn't have been able to imagine such a big-ticket item as an impulse purchase. I couldn't have imagined my husband buying a car without first talking to me either. We were a team. We made big decisions together. But David's purchase said more about our relationship with money than our relationship with each other. His new car made him smile, making me smile too. In addition to having each other, it was a luxury not to think much about money at all.

Around this same time, David gave me a nod. I then met a behind-the-scenes jeweler and selected a 1.5-carat diamond that was clearer and more perfect than the one I'd been wearing. I had the stone placed in a platinum version of the setting he had chosen, thrilled to have a ring I loved.

More than a decade later, David would hand me another velvet box, surprising me with a 3.5-carat solitaire for our twentieth wedding anniversary. I was touched he'd played the knight, giving me a bauble fit for a princess. The diamond was beautiful. But again, the real luxury was having David in my life.

Contemplation & Conversation

- Has your socioeconomic status changed? Has that change shifted the way you view yourself? What does it mean to *feel* wealthy?

- Jennifer believed that being aware and appreciative of life's abundance and remembering what mattered most would help keep her daughter from becoming spoiled. Do you agree? What do you think spoils children?

- Jennifer used wealth like a weapon at the car dealership. Does money cause obnoxious behavior?

Chapter Eight

GRATITUDE

L abor started fast on a sunny Sunday morning and required a high-speed journey down the highway to the hospital, David gripping the steering wheel and me one with the universe, singing out in soprano as each contraction hit, peaked, and passed. We pulled up to the hospital, and while David parked the car, I entered the receiving area where I rolled my head on the counter and moaned at the floor. The two women at the front desk ignored all the noise. They simply asked for my name and social security number. But when I announced a sudden need to use the restroom, they hustled me into a delivery room, and with three strong pushes, I welcomed Ali to the world.

"This is the best day of my life!" I sang out, our second daughter nestling close.

The next day, returning home, I felt the luxury of two healthy daughters, astonished at how happy Emily was to hold her baby sister. Had the two of them known one another in a past life? Emily seemed overjoyed that Ali had finally joined her, and Ali looked at home in her big sister's arms. Gazing at the two of them, I was in awe of babies, families, and life.

In the days that followed, after David was back at work, I

went into shock. An infant and a toddler were a lot of work, and Ali was a particularly fussy baby. Unlike Emily, who had been content to sit in her car seat or lounge in a bouncy chair for twenty minutes, Ali only wanted to be in my arms and cried whenever I attempted to put her down. She insisted on constant motion too, which had me swaying and bouncing through each day. Doing my best to engage with Emily too, I was often chugging through the house, Ali in my arms, Emily giggling behind me, our train circling the dining room table then moving into the living room. But when Emily got tired of being a caboose and began grabbing my legs and crying for an uppie, I often had to fight back tears. How did other mothers do it? How did they keep their sanity? My life was so easy. What was my problem?

"I'm wiped out," I said over dinner. "All day, I'm bouncing around with Ali. There's no way to get on the floor and play with Emily without Ali crying."

"We should hire a nanny," David suggested.

"A nanny? We don't need a nanny!" I snapped.

In my mind, nannies were for stuffy, conservative families that didn't care about their kids. I didn't want someone else doing the job I wanted to be doing myself.

Several years earlier, when David suggested hiring a housekeeper, my reaction had been similar. I'd felt virtue in doing chores and didn't like the idea of letting someone else do the cleaning. Growing up, I'd kept my room tidy and made my bed every day. I'd also scrubbed the bathroom my brother and I shared. It felt like my responsibility to keep the house looking great. But with the floors getting grubbier and my stress level growing, when Bill, the man who had painted the inside of our home before we moved in, told me that his wife, Noreen, was starting her own cleaning business, I broke down and hired her.

At first, I asked Noreen to come for two hours every other week. But after a couple of visits, when she let me know she needed more time to do her job well, I broke down further. What a relief! With Noreen cleaning every week for three hours, a burden was lifted. It was wonderful to return home on Tuesday evenings to a sparkling kitchen floor and a freshly vacuumed upstairs carpet calling out for bare feet.

For nearly two years, Noreen came and went like a magic fairy, doing her work at our house while I did mine at Microsoft. But the first Tuesday morning after Emily's birth, when I answered the door in my pajamas, Emily in my arms, I was shocked. There was Noreen. I'd only seen her a few times. Not only was she a real person, she reminded me of an aunt or one of my mother's friends. I welcomed her inside, and as we chatted in the hallway, my mind scanned the house, horrified at the dirty dishes in the sink and unmade bed upstairs. Noreen shouldn't be responsible for the mess I should have taken care of myself.

After that first Tuesday morning, every Monday evening, I made sure the house was in order. Then, when Noreen carted her supplies up the front steps, I did my best to stay out of her way. Actually, I did everything I could to stay out of her sight, often hiding with Emily in the nursery or going out for a walk.

"She works so hard," I told Donna. "Now that I'm home all day, I should be doing the cleaning."

"Why don't you then?"

The question was a good one, forcing me to admit my need and desire for help.

"You're right," I said. "I don't want to sweep the floor."

"Be glad you don't have to," Donna said.

"I know. I know," I said. "It just feels strange. She could be my mom."

I'd been relying on Noreen for years, but when David mentioned hiring a nanny, the rules in my head held me back, dictating that good mothers didn't let other people raise their children. With the perfect mother smiling down from her pedestal, patiently dedicating all her time to her children, I couldn't imagine being anything less, especially when I already had it too good. I wasn't deserving of yet more. I wasn't juggling two jobs or stressed about rent. I wasn't struggling with a difficult home situation. I had good friends and a loving husband. We had no financial worries and lived in a comfortable house someone else kept clean. Where was the justice in me hiring a nanny?

But with David as inseparable from Amazon as Ali was from me, evenings were tough. Most nights, he came home after Emily was in bed. To help her into her pajamas, I had to put Ali in her car seat. Then, listening to my baby cry as I helped my toddler with her pajamas, I felt those tears threatening again. With Ali back in my arms, it was Emily's turn to express her displeasure. She didn't want to get into her crib and was even less interested in having me leave the room. So, for what felt like hours, I stood in semidarkness, one hand on Emily's back, the other holding Ali.

When Emily was finally asleep, I crept downstairs to the kitchen to make dinner. Holding Ali with one hand, trying to cook with the other, I watched eight o'clock come and go. When David's key finally turned in the lock, I felt like crying once more.

"I'm exhausted. Can you hold Ali?" I asked.

"Can you at least say hello when I walk in the door?" he growled. "I don't feel very welcomed. I need ten minutes to relax."

"Ten minutes!" I barked back. "I've been waiting for hours! You've had ten minutes. You had all day to yourself. You just had time alone in the car."

"I'm so glad I hurried home. It's great to be here."

"Great to have you," I snapped, taking Ali upstairs.

With my husband's stress colliding with mine, I turned to Carla and Grace. Although our PEPS group had disbanded, the three of us were still meeting every week, communing over the joys and trials of parenthood. We routinely discussed strained relationships and the chronic condition of being too tired to think. But while a juicy story about a horrible husband would be good fodder for a morning chat, I didn't want to gripe and complain. I wanted advice.

"Get some help," Carla said. "I would if I could."

I smiled. But I didn't believe her. Carla wouldn't hire someone to take care of her son. She was a dedicated mother.

"I don't know," I said. "I've never imagined having a nanny. I want to be with Emily and Ali. I like being a mom."

"Don't worry. You'll still be a mom," Carla said with a laugh.

"It's ridiculous," I said. "I'm not even working. My life is so easy. I can't get more help."

"Lose the guilt," Grace told me. "You look exhausted."

That night, seeking more reassurance, I asked David if he thought I was a good mother.

"You're a wonderful mom," he said. "But maybe you'd be an even better one if you hired someone to help you."

"What about the girls? Won't they miss out?" I asked. "I don't want to miss out on them. I'll lose something if we hire a nanny."

"Yeah, the grouchiness," he said with a chuckle. "You can't cherry-pick your experience. The relationship you have with Emily and Ali might not be the same if we hire a nanny, but that's okay. Maybe your relationship with the girls would be even better."

Luckily, Donna came to my rescue. Pregnant with her second child, on the verge of leaving Microsoft, and concerned about being at home with an infant and a toddler herself, she wanted part-time help—and her need allowed me to justify my own. What's more, as we talked about hiring a nanny together and providing someone a full-time job, I could imagine the balance sheet in the sky finding some equilibrium.

As soon as Donna and I placed an advertisement in the *Seattle Times*, seeking a nanny to be shared between our two families, we found the ideal candidate in Amy, a recent college graduate with a teaching degree. Young and upbeat, Amy had moved to Seattle from Madison, Wisconsin, planning to teach fourth grade. But she'd arrived too late in the hiring cycle to get a position in the public schools and had been considering substitute teaching when she saw our advertisement.

On the first afternoon Amy was scheduled to start work, I walked through the living room, straightening books into piles.

Then, when Amy arrived, I introduced her to Emily and Ali and suggested a trip to the park. Once there, hoping Amy knew her presence was justified, as she pushed Emily on a swing and I bounced around with Ali, I rattled on about how hard David worked and how impossible it was to make dinner.

"It will be nice to spend quality, one-on-one time with each of the girls," I told her.

I didn't want Amy to think I was avoiding my children. I didn't want her to question my need. Nor did I want her to see me as interested in just going to lunch with friends and getting my nails done.

Back home, although tempted to continue building my case as a good, responsible mother, I forced myself upstairs, stopping on the landing, braced for Ali's cry. But Ali was fine. Emily was too. So was Amy.

Standing in the bedroom, I whispered into the phone to Donna.

"Amy seems great, but it's awkward. It's weird having her here. I don't know what to do. I'm scared to go downstairs."

"What? Why?" Donna asked.

"I don't want Amy to think I'm just sitting around. It's not like I can just go downstairs and look at magazines."

"Why not? Do you want to come over here and watch my kids? I wouldn't mind reading a magazine."

"I'd actually like to cook dinner. But it doesn't feel right to play in the kitchen when my babies are in the living room with a stranger."

"They're fine," Donna said. "Go downstairs. Make dinner. Enjoy yourself."

I hung up and eased my way to the first floor, sliding into the kitchen to slice mushrooms and whisk eggs for a frittata. Absorbed in the preparation, I was beginning to enjoy the process of cooking dinner when my inner critic started at me again, demanding to know why I wasn't a more attentive mother. I then imagined Amy's voice calling out from the living room, wondering why rich people didn't like being with their children.

Amy had only been working for our family a few weeks when I asked her to join us in Florence, Italy, hoping the trip I'd planned might actually be a vacation if I had help. Thankfully, Donna agreed to let Amy come with us. Amy was excited too. She'd spent a semester in Italy during college and was eager to return.

On a late September evening, Amy and our family landed in Florence and drove into the countryside where we bumped along dirt roads for an hour before stopping in front of a massive stone villa. As we got out of the car and admired the view, an older woman pulled up on a black bicycle. She introduced herself as Mrs. Bianca, then bustled into the house to prepare our evening meal.

When David had suggested hiring a chef, I hadn't been interested in having someone else do something I liked doing myself. There was no reason for a chef. I was capable, competent, and liked to cook. But with encouragement, I'd agreed to get help. And after fourteen hours of travel, it was a relief to take a shower and not think about what to make for dinner. Even more wonderful was hearing Ms. Bianca call us to the table. She served up a meal made with tomatoes so fresh, basil so fragrant, and penne so perfectly done that we couldn't stop eating. Just as Amy was spooning a third helping of pasta into Emily's bowl, more food arrived. Excited, we dug into chicken fricassee with sage and a leafy green salad dressed in olive oil and salt, grateful for Mrs. Bianca and her artistry in the kitchen.

After that first dinner, I asked Mrs. Bianca if she could return every night. She nodded in agreement, then used her shoulders and upturned palms to ask what we wanted her to prepare. Our Italian was as limited as her English, and as David began to moo like a cow, and I made lips like a fish, it was clear Mrs. Bianca should decide—and we weren't disappointed. With the face of an apple doll and a can-do spirit, Mrs. Bianca arrived every afternoon on her bicycle, bags of fresh produce heaped on the back. She put on her apron, and without a word, made one delicious meal after the next, going through a full bottle of olive oil and pounds of pasta during our stay.

Not only did I welcome Mrs. Bianca to the house every afternoon, over the course of the vacation, I became increasingly appreciative of Amy's help. As a breastfeeding woman with two kids in diapers, I couldn't stop bare bottoms and boobs from flying in all directions. And when Amy got a chance sighting of David and me dashing naked from the kitchen to the bedroom, all was exposed. Amy saw me at my grumpiest and most disheveled. She witnessed me sitting around doing nothing. And to my surprise, she didn't turn away in disgust. In fact, perhaps more aware of just how much she was needed, she seemed to find more satisfaction in her job. An infant and a toddler were a lot of work. I was exhausted and overwhelmed. I was also humbled, truly grateful to have Amy with us.

One afternoon, I was sitting in a park, watching David and

the girls play on the swings, when an American man rushed over and dropped a box of toys in my lap. He told me he couldn't bring the toys with him on his flight home and hoped our family would enjoy them. Before I could stop him, or even think to thank him, he was gone. Immediately, I looked around for another family more deserving of the gift. We already had way more than our share. We couldn't accept yet more. But then, looking down at the big glassy eyes of the stuffed dog in my lap, patting the fuzzy head and smoothing the floppy ears, I felt the thoughtfulness of a stranger, and those tears threatened again. Our wealth didn't stop me from needing to squeeze a stuffed animal. Money didn't keep me from being overwhelmed—and my heart opened to accept the gift.

Over a decade later, interviewing people who had more money than they had growing up, I felt a similar sense of relief and gratitude. Other people shared my insecurities and mixed emotions. Talking about situations that arose and hearing other people's thoughts and ideas helped demystify wealth. We all had concerns around hiring people, raising children, and giving to charity. It was validating and cathartic to discuss feelings of guilt and pride. Breaking the silence confirmed the importance of sharing stories and finding connections. We all had parents, siblings, and friends. If we talked more openly, maybe we could take the power away from money. By staying quiet, we were allowing society to continue glorifying and demonizing wealth, which only perpetuated divides. Were we hiding behind wealth?

When I asked about hiring help and paying for personal services, the people I talked to acknowledged the emotional complexity and challenge of navigating relationships that were neither purely business nor just personal.

Julie, whose husband had a highly successful career in finance, found she took on the problems of the people who worked for her.

"It can get complicated," she said. "Our housekeeper's apartment building caught fire, so we put her up in a hotel. I think she had a lot of people staying with her because the TV got damaged. The hotel charged us. Of course, we paid, but it was awkward to get that call and to talk to our housekeeper about the situation. She was embarrassed."

Nicole, a corporate real estate developer, couldn't bring herself to let go of her nanny even though her oldest was in college and two younger children were in high school.

"She's been with us for twenty-one years," Nicole said. "I don't need her anymore, but I can't bring myself to cut down her hours. She needs the job."

Most of the people I spoke with were in positions of power over the people who worked for them, but one newly wealthy woman felt the imbalance in reverse.

"The household manager we hired was twenty years older than me and had worked for wealthy families for decades. She knew more about being rich than I did. It was embarrassing to be told I need to buy new silverware."

The same woman had hired a chef to make dinner for her family twice a week while she was at work but her nanny and the chef weren't getting along.

"I've been coming home from work to find them fighting," she said. "It's so stressful. I'm not sure what to do."

Another woman, Betsy, who had worked in finance but had been outside of the workforce for years, told me she was planning to take a new job.

"My husband wants me to hire a household manager," she said. "But I don't want someone poking around in my business. I like my privacy." After a few moments, she asked, "What exactly does a household manager do anyway?"

The question was reasonable. And yet, both of us laughed, embarrassed not to know, as though having wealth meant our knowledge of such things should be complete and automatic. Neither of us understood the responsibilities of a household manager or why exactly people hired one—and again it was clear that talking was helpful. In fact, I got an answer from Mary, who'd had a household manager for years and let me know how much she appreciated having someone else run errands, pay bills, call repairmen, walk the dog, and do the grocery shopping while she concentrated on her career.

Seeing my world through Amy's eyes, I was even more aware of the relative ease and advantages in my life, which had me keeping my voice low when making airline reservations over the phone, worried Amy would hear how much we were spending. I made a point of throwing grocery bills away and didn't let tags from clothes sit around on the dresser. I also took shopping bags upstairs and hid them in the closet. Amy didn't need to know the price of my jeans or that I'd purchased another pair of shoes. But I wasn't fooling anyone. Amy was aware of the imbalance. She was also a source of joy to Emily and Ali and a huge support to me. I was thankful to have time to go out for a run, and do the grocery shopping on my own. I was also happy to return home to the sound of Amy and the girls laughing upstairs.

When Amy took a job as a fourth-grade teacher, Donna and I were both happy for her, but sad to see her go. Aware of how much a nanny meant to us, we agreed we wanted to hire someone else together—and pay our next nanny more. Not only could we both afford the expense, we wanted to be generous, perhaps help narrow that gap. It may have been tempting to think of our nanny as part of the family, especially since the relationship was so close. But it wasn't easy to watch other people's kids. Being a nanny was a job. Donna and I were employers. And knowing that our nanny would be spending time in our homes, involved in our personal affairs, privy to the intimate details of our lives, we wanted to make sure our next nanny felt part of the action, not resentful.

"We should pay more than the going rate," I said. "But how much?"

"It's hard to know the right amount," Donna said.

We wanted our nanny's salary to be above and beyond what most nannies made, but we wanted to be businesslike and professional too. We weren't interested in grossly overpaying. With no one to talk to, no way to discuss our goal, it was hard to determine how much would ensure our next nanny felt respected as an employee and grateful to have found us.

After much deliberation, with no outside information, we decided on a salary that was twenty-five percent higher than we'd paid Amy. We looked to the Microsoft model too, planning to give our next nanny performance reviews, salary increases, and bonuses every six months. Then, with a strategy in place, when I ran into a woman named May, who had worked at Emily's old daycare and was in-between jobs, I knew exactly who to hire. May was easygoing and had a gentle, caring attitude. She loved to be with children and liked the idea of working for two families rather than at another daycare. But she didn't have a car.

"Maybe we should just buy her one," Donna said. "My neighbor has an old Honda Accord he wants to sell. He's meticulous. I bet it's in great shape."

At first, I couldn't imagine buying a car for our nanny. Just saying the words made my eyes roll. Who could do such a thing? But excited about hiring May, Donna and I ended up purchasing Donna's neighbor's twelve-year-old Honda Accord and giving it to May to use on the job.

If I'd still been self-conscious about our money, wrapped up in guilt, aiming for perfection, or unable to accept help, there'd have been no way to justify the car. I couldn't have hired another nanny either. But more grateful for the abundance in my life, I let money make my life easier. It made May's life easier too. In fact, the more I embraced and appreciated my own privilege and freedom, the more I wanted to share it.

After only a few weeks of letting May drive the Honda on the job, Donna and I told her she could drive the car home. Eventually, we would sell her the car for a dollar. At the time, more aware of my good fortune, I told Noreen I wanted to pay her half again as much as she was already making. It felt great to acknowledge and reward her good work. There was a ripple effect too. My belief in Noreen and willingness to compensate her for her thoroughness, efficiency, and great attitude boosted her confidence, compelling her to ask other clients for a pay increase too. It was gratifying to see her standing up for herself and getting paid what she deserved. And yet, I was aware of the downside. My ability to pay clearly impacted others. While Noreen benefited and some of her clients were likely happy to give her a raise, others might not have been pleased. For example, some of the women in Emily's co-op preschool might have had a hard time paying more.

At a recent co-op preschool meeting, when the conversation turned to date night and how much to pay the babysitter, I again found myself staying quiet.

"How much do you pay?" someone asked.

"We have a high school girl who sits for us once a week," one woman said. "We pay her seven dollars an hour."

"Do you think I need to pay a college student more? It's hard to know the right amount."

One woman suggested asking the college student what she charged. Another recommended paying eight dollars an hour and giving a nice tip. Someone else advised a flat rate of ten dollars an hour. It was good to hear women talking about money, benefitting from each other's knowledge and advice. And as I thought about how hard it had been for Donna and me to decide how much to pay May, I wanted to share my story. We were all trying to figure out the right amount to pay the people who looked after our kids. I was grateful to have a housekeeper and help with the girls and to be able to compensate them well. I was also grateful David could buy a car on a whim, and I could buy a car for our nanny. The amount I was paying may have been higher, but the questions we were all asking were similar.

Like most people, Donna and I wanted to be generous and businesslike, to pay an amount that fit our budget and the job being done. But, worried that some might only hear me talking about our wealth, my attempt to draw parallels falling flat, I kept my story to myself.

Contemplation & Conversation

- Do you have household help? What is your relationship with the people who work for you? Do you try to hide what you have?

- Do you think Jennifer should have given her housekeeper a pay increase when it meant other people would have to pay more as well?

- Should Jennifer have shared her story about buying a car for her nanny? What do you think would have happened if she did?

Chapter Nine

AN EDUCATION

rivate preschool hadn't been part of my childhood. At five years old, I walked down the street, crossed with a guard, and went to kindergarten with other children from the neighborhood. Since David had attended his local public elementary school too, we'd both assumed Emily and Ali would do the same. We wanted to be good local citizens, supporting our city's schools, and having our children go to class nearby. But when we talked with a friend who was a teacher at an elementary school close to our house, our ideals and advantages collided with the reality of the public system.

"There's a real shortage," she said.

"Not enough money?" I asked.

"Not enough paper. Every teacher gets one ream for the semester. When it runs out, things get nasty. People start stealing . . . not the students, the teachers. It's hard to focus on my class when I have to lock up my stuff so another teacher doesn't take it."

Hearing this, I looked into independent elementary schools with preschool programs—and entered a foreign land. Every school boasted small class sizes and excellent teachers. They all had innovative curricula and creative teaching methods. Children in attendance were blossoming as individuals and thriving within groups. It all seemed too good to be true. For many, it was. The cost was outrageous. And yet, with Emily staring up at me, eager and ready to learn, like any parent, I wanted to do what was best for my child.

Unwilling to sacrifice Emily's education for the good of a broken public system, I joined other highly advantaged, overly involved mothers and fathers in a competition that had nothing to do with the good of the whole, and everything to do with determination and wealth. Just applying to an independent preschool was like attending boot camp, making me painfully aware that we were living in a small corner of the world, unfairly privileged. Independent schools were a glaring example of inequality. But even as I labeled the system problematic and the process unfair, I played the game. I took tours, attended information sessions, signed up for interviews, filled out lengthy written applications, and clearly acted out of self-interest, using the resources at my disposal—money, connections, and time— to get Emily into the "right" place.

When I was touring one of the schools that seemed like a good fit for Emily, a pregnant woman on the tour told me she had been a student at the school herself and would do anything to get her unborn child into the preschool class in five years. Hearing this, rather than shaking my head at the craziness or shrugging, unaffected, I felt an increased panic. When it came to Emily, the stakes were high. If she didn't get into the right preschool program at a good elementary school, she might not be accepted at a strong middle school, might not attend a great high school, and might not go to a top college on the path to an enriching career.

Looking back, I wished my attitude had been more relaxed. I could have avoided all the pressure parents put on themselves and their children if I'd truly kept Emily top-of-mind. My goal was for her to be happy and fulfilled. I wanted her to feel good about herself, to be a motivated, contributing member of society. But instead of backing off with enlightened awareness, I launched myself into the fray of preschool applications, driven by the fear of missing out and the desire to look like a good parent, telling myself I was doing it all for Emily.

After considering several independent schools, David and I applied to University Child Development School. UCDS honored individual learning styles and had multiage classrooms where students learned from one another. The facilities were under construction and a couple of classes were held in temporary, portable units, but the facilities themselves weren't as important to us as a collaborative, supportive environment. The teachers seemed happy. The students looked happy too. So, after reviewing the parent application, I set to work answering questions. What are your child's favorite activities when alone? How would you describe your child's sense of humor, both verbal and nonverbal? What situations frustrate your child? How does your child's curiosity show itself? About what types of things does your child wonder?

In addition to the written application and parent interview, like many other schools, UCDS required children to attend a play day. It was hard to imagine how a three-year-old would spend an hour and a half in an unknown place, sharing nicely with other children and listening attentively to the teachers. Instead of letting the day unfold, I began regulating Emily's naps and meals, doing my best to ensure she was well-fed, well-rested, and ready to impress. Then, on the afternoon of the play day, aware of being way too worked up, I sat for a moment in the car in front of UCDS and took a couple of deep breaths. Once I was feeling calmer, I helped Emily out of her car seat and together we walked across the parking lot. But my calm vanished when we ran into Melinda Gates and her daughter, who was applying as well.

Later, when I returned to the school, Emily was beaming. She handed me her artwork, told me about ladybug day, and led me to the terrarium to see the insects. The teachers were smiling too. They confirmed we would be receiving a letter in the spring. Hearing this, I thought Emily had aced the test, our family accepted. Four months later, however, when cold, rainy March crept into view, we got a revealingly thin envelope.

The school told us Emily wasn't ready for a half-day class, but I wasn't convinced. Searching for the *real* reason our daughter hadn't been accepted, I questioned what had happened during the play day and suspected David of being too aggressive with his questions at our parent interview. In the past, I might have blamed money, believing "the rich" were using their wealth to buy their way in. Perhaps it was true. In the future, I would again be painfully aware that the private school system was rigged in favor of those with resources. At the same time, while some made huge donations at questionable moments, most people played within the rules.

At the time, instead of worrying myself into a future of college rejections, I finally saw our daughter. She was sitting at her pink table, her feet dangling above the ground as she drew big-headed stick people and smiling yellow suns. She didn't need to compete with other children to prove she was lovable. She didn't have to achieve and accomplish to feel okay about herself. She was happy to be at home, contributing as an artist. What was I thinking? Emily didn't have to attend the right preschool to have a happy life and be a contributing member of society.

When Emily was a year older, and I'd matured by another year as well, we revisited a few independent schools, considered the Waldorf, Montessori, and public options, but agreed that UCDS was the place we liked the best. Again, I toured the school, attended another information session, and took Emily to a play day. Six months later, when UCDS mailed acceptances to the half-day preschool class, we received a thick folder.

With Emily's formal education about to begin, my education continued. Independent schools were not as they'd appeared from the outside looking in. There were unexpected challenges and rituals, again proving we had entered a foreign land. For one, the stated $10,000 was not the real price for a three-hour-a-day preschool class. The tuition we were paying supposedly didn't cover the cost of running the school. Donations were expected. Actually, contributions of thousands of dollars were practically required. Even more bewildering, while David and I listened to the head of school welcome new families and tell us we needed to make meaningful gifts, no one flinched. No waves of disbelief rippled along the rows. No one left the room or cried out in despair. How did so many parents know what to expect? Were they just staying quiet? Most parents were like us, new to the world of independent schools and without experience. But no one was walking away. No one was talking either.

The late-breaking news of the school's expectations was a surprise to David and me but must have been a deal-breaker for others. Carla, my friend from PEPS was in shock. She and her husband had accepted a preschool spot for their son at an independent school on the other side of the city, but after he'd been in class a few weeks, she wasn't sure he could stay.

"I feel pressure to give something we just don't have," Carla said. "I don't want to be a social outcast at the school. None of the other parents seem to even notice the expense or have a problem paying."

I empathized with Carla. In fact, in affinity with her, I wanted to discuss the issue further, but I was afraid to talk about finances. I didn't want to put our friendship at risk. And as I avoided the subject, Carla did too. Meanwhile, at UCDS, I slipped into line, accepting the new norm without saying a word. Again, it didn't feel appropriate to talk about money. In part, I was still competing. I didn't want to appear inexperienced or ignorant about how independent schools worked. Talking about money would have gotten me off to the wrong start, labeling me as inappropriate and naïve. But in my silence, I was again contributing to an unfair system that wasn't working well for anyone.

With so many privileged, highly successful families together in one place, perhaps it shouldn't have been a surprise that the rivalry that had existed during the application process hadn't been left at the door. Most parents were nice, and Emily liked her classmates, but there was a lot of posturing as parents sized up one another, flaunting high-powered business careers, work in law firms or private medical practices, and positions on non-profit boards. Most had money and time to spare, and since expensive homes, luxury cars, and exotic travel were givens, competition existed in the details—and my mania for holiday cards began.

Christmas greetings had been in my life for years, a nice way to connect with old friends and extended family. But as an independent school parent, trying to be part of the in-crowd, I didn't just purchase boxes of cards. I found a custom card shop and hired a professional photographer. I then dressed the girls in cute outfits and jumped around, trying to get them to smile at the right moment and at the same time. There was no Face-book, Instagram, or photocard services, and since no one had yet begun sending photographs of their families, my efforts paid off with uniquely impressive greetings. But over the next few years, as we began receiving photocards from other families, my desire to improve upon each previous year's card turned my stomach to knots. Starting in October, I kept my fingers crossed for good moods all around during our photo shoot. Once candid pictures had been taken and the best one selected, I spent weeks coming up with a clever way to let everyone know another year had been happily overachieved, exotic vacations enjoyed.

Holiday cards aside, I wanted to get involved at Emily's school, but it wasn't easy. There was a questionnaire included in the school's welcome packet asking parents to list the skills and talents they could contribute to the auction taking place in the spring. But after Emily had been in school a few weeks, I realized filling out a form distributed by the administration was not actually the way to volunteer. I had to get to know the influencers and decision makers within the parent community.

"The other parents are nice, but the auction is out of control," I told my friend, Leslie, who lived in New York City. "There's a competition to volunteer. New parents get the worst jobs, if they get to help at all."

"Welcome to the world of high-pressure schools. Sounds typical of schools here," Leslie said. "Just wait until the holidays. At our school, there's always a competition around teachers' gifts."

"What do you mean?"

"Everyone looks around to see how much each family is spending on the teachers. We all want to know who is giving the nicest gifts. We watch the two or three richest families to see what they'll do."

"That's awful."

"Actually, it's fascinating."

"It sounds like a competition between the parents, and not a gift for the teachers."

"Teachers win in the end. They know how much these families have and are hoping for a share in the wealth. They deserve it."

"Come on," I said. "The teachers aren't judging their gifts."

"Be realistic," Leslie said. "When the teachers at your school figure out you guys are loaded, they'll expect, or at least hope, you give them something big."

"I'm not sure how holiday gifts are handled at Emily's school," I said. "I hope parents pool their money and buy a gift together.

Do you really think people are thinking about what everyone has and what gift they are giving?"

The pitch of Leslie's voice rose. "Are you kidding? Of course they are. And you should give more than other people. I'm not trying to make you feel bad. I'm just telling you the way people see things. They have expectations. Maybe you should think about why this gets you so worked up. I'm surprised it's an issue."

It was an issue. And when I hung up, I thought the issue was Leslie's. She was so preoccupied with money. But as I fumed about her warped sense of reality, I thought back to a wedding gift we'd received from Microsoft friends, and realized I was guilty of exactly what Leslie was describing. Opening that gift and seeing a simple wooden picture frame, I'd been upset our rich friends were being so cheap. Aware of their wealth, I'd been hoping for something significant.

Leslie was right. People had expectations. And from within a small corner of the world, as a member of an independent school community, it was clear I had become one of *those people*. My responsibility and obligation to give back was clear as well.

Contemplation & Conversation

- Jennifer believes our education system doesn't work well for anyone. What are your thoughts? What could individuals do to help?

- Parents at Emily's new independent school competed with one another. Is there competition at your child's school? How does that competition show itself?

Chapter Ten

WITHIN OUR MEANS

In 1999, Amazon's founder and CEO, Jeff Bezos, was *Time* magazine's Man of the Year, the Amazon stock price was sky-rocketing, and the dot-com boom was ushering mega yachts, private jets, and IPOs into our nation's collective consciousness. Later, our country's fascination with wealth would have us following the Kardashians, adoring Downton Abbey, and loving to hate the one percent. At the time, we were watching Paris Hilton, both appalled and intrigued.

Given all the shimmer and shine associated with wealth, I felt dull. We weren't living the way "the rich" supposedly lived. Our life was far from newsworthy. David was working twelve-hour days while I stayed home with the girls in our family-friendly neighborhood, both of us driving cars that didn't stand out from any others on the street. There were no fountains of champagne or wild parties in our lives, no sweeping staircases, no crystal chandeliers, no staff attending to our every need. What were we doing with all our money? Why exactly weren't we taking more advantage of our good fortune? Without an answer, and again hoping to make a change and have more fun, I resolved to start "doing rich right."

At first, I looked to our friends. With Lynn and Adam in the process of furnishing a second house on Lopez Island, three hours from Seattle, and Donna and Matt about to put an offer on a vacation place in Sun Valley, Idaho, I wondered if we should be considering a second home. But my understanding of vacation places was limited. Didn't they eat up every scrap of a family's money and energy? I didn't want to feel tied down or give up on trips to other places.

"We can travel as usual," David told me. "A second place will give us options, not limit the possibilities."

Considering where we enjoyed spending time, Napa Valley became our goal. We'd visited with Donna and Matt when all of us were single, returned as married couples, and had gone back together with infants and toddlers. The food and wine were delicious and the atmosphere magical.

In March 2000, after the world had successfully entered the twenty-first century without an electronic collapse, when Emily was beginning to speak in short sentences, Ali was crawling, and the dot-com bubble was at its very fattest, I contacted a realtor. Several weeks later, he called me back.

"There's an 1899 Victorian you might want to see," he said. "It's not officially on the market, but the owners may be interested in selling."

David and I flew down and toured the house. Then, with a lot less thought and a lot more money than we'd employed in the purchase of our first house in Seattle five years earlier, we bought our second place for nearly two million dollars. Over Memorial Day weekend, and again for the Fourth of July, our family camped on mattresses in the empty living room and played in the pool.

As fall approached, ready to embark upon what Microsoft friends had been doing for years, I interviewed architects and contractors, planning for a massive remodel. Perfectly arranged rooms and designer furniture had never been part of my life, but given our resources and my resolution, I wanted to hire an interior designer too. Luckily, I found Cheryl. Or perhaps, she found me.

A decorator from San Francisco, Cheryl told me over the phone that she listened closely to every client and adapted to any taste. When we met at the house a few weeks later, she strode through the door in crisp beige linen and orange eyeglasses, proving to have a distinctive style of her own.

"Great place," she drawled, looking up at the ceiling. "Good height."

Cheryl gave a nod to the wraparound front porch and spacious rooms and wasn't bashful about which walls needed to come down and where additional windows were required. As we discussed opening up the back of the house to connect the interior with the outdoors and contemplated raising the ceiling in the stairwell to bring in more light, we became a team.

Several months after hiring Cheryl, I flew to San Francisco to meet with her and her associate, Marla. Listening to the stylish duo talk about antiques sourced from Paris and projects in Sun Valley, I was intimidated by their ability to spend big. Could I harness their high-end influence? Would they shamelessly overspend? We didn't want a home that was formal or flashy. We wanted to create spaces that were accessible, where we could spend time as a family and with friends. Cheryl and Marla nodded. Then, touring the designer showrooms, looking at textiles and fixtures, tiles and tubs, embracing my resolution, I began having fun.

By March 2003, our remodel was nearly complete, and for a night, while the girls stayed home with May in Seattle, David and I flew down to walk through the house with the contractor. The construction team had done great work, and with painting set to begin the following month and a furniture delivery date on the calendar, we were on track for completion by the end of June. Later in the evening, however, when we returned to the house and stood alone in the backyard, we began to pick at imperfections.

"I don't like the pool house," David said. "It's too big. It's overshadowing the backyard."

"We already approved it," I said. "The construction is complete."

"They need to tear it down. The scale is wrong."

The next day, when I talked to the contractor about making a change, he explained that the best approach would be to lift the whole structure off the ground and cut a foot off around the bottom.

"The windows will be closer to the floor than intended," he said. "But you'll hardly notice. This way, you'll spend a lot less than if you take off the roof."

"See. Anything can be done," David said with a grin.

"That's good," I said. "Because we have to do something about the pool."

A new pool had been installed but when we walked into the finished shell, I was worried about the girls.

"It's way too deep," I said.

"Depth is good," David argued. "When the girls are in their teens, they'll want to dive."

"They have to live that long," I countered. "We have toddlers. We need a shallower pool."

It wasn't possible to reduce the depth by adding a layer of concrete to the finished shell. The whole structure had to be drilled apart, additional rebar installed. And with the contractor telling me he could get started right away, I was beginning to think money had the power to fix any problem.

◆　◆　◆

In 2002, the closest David and I had come to a private jet was reading about corrupt business executives using shareholders' money to fly girlfriends to Miami and the family dog to the lake house. But after traveling on Amazon business in Jeff's private plane, David couldn't wait to charter a jet for our family. There was no way to justify the expense, but he claimed we'd save time.

"It's so much more efficient," David said.

After years of being fascinated by cars, trains, and flying machines, David wanted to have an adventure in the air.

"You just drive up and walk on board," he said. "There's no wait, no line, no metal detector."

In the past, I would have pushed back, uncomfortable with the extravagance, but having made my resolution to do rich right, it was hard not to admit being curious. Soon, we were exiting the highway several miles before the airport, zipping along a narrow two-lane road, and turning into a small parking lot. A sleek white jet was a few hundred yards away, its staircase extended, a man in uniform standing in the doorway, looking as though he were expecting someone important. But he wasn't. He was waiting for us.

We crossed the tarmac, dragging two suitcases, a portable crib, a stroller, and two children's backpacks, all of which another uniformed man took from us at the bottom of the stairs.

"What big girls," the pilot declared, smiling at Emily and Ali. "Are you looking forward to the flight?"

"Sure am!" I said, ducking into the cabin, realizing too late he wasn't talking to me.

The interior was tan. Gold-rimmed lights dotted the ceiling and two panels of highly polished wood slid along each wall. Stroking the pleated leather seats, I made my way toward the back and opened the door to the lavatory, which boasted a gold sink and gold faucets.

"Can I sit by the window?" Emily asked.

With four puckered leather loungers, a matching loveseat, and windows on either side, it was hard not to get a window seat.

"You can sit anywhere you like," I told her.

Emily scrambled into a chair. Ali sat next to her. And after buckling the girls in, I took the spot across the aisle from David, who was smiling broadly. He gave the pilot an authoritative thumbs up and we took off.

Several months after that inaugural flight, David suggested

hiring another jet for a weekend vacation to Santa Barbara with Donna and her family.

"We'll need a larger plane," he said. "And a flight attendant."

The eight of us were soon crossing the tarmac and ascending the retractable stairs. Inside, the children jumped around and giggled at the toilet while Donna, Matt, David and I took our places, David and me glowing and Donna and Matt impressed. Flying alone as a family had been an experience, but flying with friends allowed us to show off. In fact, on the return trip, when Donna told us she had business in Portland the following day, David asked the pilot to make an unplanned stop to drop her off.

◆ ◆ ◆

On the morning of my thirty-fifth birthday, a gift from David was waiting on the doorstep: a dark-haired woman, wearing cropped jeans and a sheer black top was peering through the screen looking as though she had just taken a yellow cab straight from Manhattan, a foil balloon bobbing incongruously behind her and a single-layer birthday cake scrawled with pink and yellow frosting balanced in one hand. Part of the fashion-forward scene from Mario's, a high-end clothing store in downtown Seattle where clients ordered Prada boots in early spring and Dolce & Gabbana flew out the door year-round, Joan was going to help me put together a new wardrobe. Her mission for the morning was to go through my closet, assess my holdings, and discard the undesirable. In two days, she would meet Donna and me in San Francisco for a day of extreme shopping.

"Happy birthday," she said, handing me the cake.

I directed Joan upstairs to our bedroom and into my closet, where she stopped and inhaled, but didn't pause for long. Her hands were soon sweeping over my clothes, her eyes scanning my shoes while she pulled pants from hangers and threw shirts and dresses onto the bed. In twenty minutes, my entire wardrobe was spread across the room, and decisions needed to be made.

"We'll look at each item and touch it only once," Joan announced. She pointed to a pair of black pants that zipped at the side. "Let me see those on you."

I tried on the pants as Joan asked about my favorite outfit. When I told her how much I loved my light blue flowery capris and blue knit top with three-quarter-length sleeves, she pinched her chin.

"Fine for trips to the park with the kids," she said, "but we can do better."

Joan nodded at my black pants.

"The fit is good," she said. "Let's put together some outfits."

Joan chose a blouse, then another, suggesting combinations I'd never tried. She looked through my sweaters, declaring some outdated and others as having potential if paired with the right jeans.

"You have some nice pieces," she informed me. "We can work with a lot of this."

I tried on a dress I hadn't worn in years while Joan watched.

"Too snug. Recycle," she commanded.

I'd imagined awkward moments, but with an authority figure sanctioning indulgence and vanity, it was fun to look through all my clothes, and evaluate what I had. Standing in front of the mirror in my underwear, thinking about all the new outfits Joan was helping me put together, I believed "fabulous" just might become my middle name, and couldn't wait to go shopping with Donna.

Prancing happily out of the morning in my favorite flowery capris and top with three-quarter-length sleeves, thanking Joan for her time, I wasn't bothered when she said, "You're wearing *that* on your birthday?" The experience had made me feel like a million bucks.

The next afternoon, Donna and I flew first class to San Francisco and checked into a five-star hotel where I drifted to sleep with visions of high-heeled pumps and ribbed cotton sweaters dancing in my head. Joan arrived on a separate flight and met us for coffee the following morning.

"We're going to a small boutique on Sacramento," she announced. "They're expecting us."

Leaning back in her chair and looking directly at me, she added, "I figured you had some bank when your husband called."

Kicking Donna under the table, I tried not to laugh. Her comment was comical. Was she talking about me?

"Get ready to drop some dough," she continued as we got in a taxi.

Who knows what she told the women at the boutique? When we arrived, they were overjoyed to see us, calling me by name and offering Perrier to everyone. At first, looking at the array of color-coordinated clothing, I wanted one of everything. But working my way systematically along the rows of browns and oranges, blues and greens, I got pickier, selecting a pair of wide-legged wool pants, a knee-length skirt, two cashmere sweaters, and a short-sleeved silk blouse. The saleswomen praised my good taste and carried my chosen items to the back while Donna made suggestions and Joan selected a few pieces as well. Finally, I made my way to the dressing room and one of the saleswomen drew a heavy velvet curtain in a semicircle around me.

In junior high, I'd shopped with my mother, the two of us spending hours in cramped quarters with scuffed walls and built-in benches. My mom was often perched in a corner, holding clothes and hangers on her lap, while I struggled to find jeans that fit and weren't too expensive. Back-to-school shopping meant purchasing a couple of shirts and pairs of pants. It was always tough to decide what to take home and what to leave behind. Now, cloaked within a massive curtain, standing before a gilded mirror, four women at my service, no one limiting my spending—not even me—I had become Cinderella.

"Those brown slacks would look great with that orange cashmere sweater," Donna said.

"They'll need to be cinched at the waist," Joan stated. "What a great basic."

Joan requested a tailor, who appeared minutes later, pinned the waist on the pants and marked three other pairs to be hemmed. Meanwhile, after disappearing, Joan returned with several colorful silk blouses.

"These are perfect for a dinner with girlfriends," she said. "Each one makes a statement without being too trendy. Good with jeans. Good with skirts or slacks. I insist. These are must-have pieces for your fall closet."

I stepped out of the dressing room, believing the right look would soon be mine, and added two $290 silk blouses, an orange cashmere Loro Piana sweater for $450, a paisley Etro shirt for $350, a flowing black $650 Prada skirt, and a pair of $800 Manolo Blahnik heels to the stack of clothes already waiting at the register. As the saleswoman rang up my purchases, I looked through some pashminas neatly folded on the counter. Holding up a beaded maroon wrap, I looked over at Donna who nodded. And when Joan proclaimed beading in for the fall, resolved to do rich right, I tossed the wrap onto the pile destined for Seattle, adding $350 to my bill.

We left the store and Donna turned to me.

"Good work! You got some great things."

"Thanks," I said. "And thanks for being here."

Having Donna with me as confidante and cheerleader reminded me of all the times we'd shopped together in high school, spending hours at the mall, wrangling with racks and rummaging through bins. We'd loved the challenge of finding sweaters and shirts at a discount. It was exciting to discover a great pair of jeans marked down 50 percent. We never paid full price. Neither of us could afford it. But even if we could have, finding deals was fun.

Leaving the boutique having paid full price for everything, I felt a twinge of discontent. With helpful saleswomen catering to my needs, the experience of shopping was not at all the same as it had been in high school. Instead of being involved physically and emotionally, making tough decisions, I was at a distance. With next season's styles lined up in front of me, I only needed to point and nod. No trade-offs were required. Given Joan's guidance, I didn't even need good taste.

"Let's go," Joan said.

Snapping out of reminiscing about the past, I jumped into the taxi Joan had waved down. We were heading to Neiman Marcus.

"We're getting your eyebrows waxed," Joan told me.

"Sounds good," I said with a laugh.

Were my brows that bad? Did we have time to fix them? Our return flight was in three hours, and I needed an evening bag and high-heeled pumps.

At Neiman's, we cruised through the accessories, stopping in handbags where I lingered over a gorgeous Fendi purse. It was just what I wanted. But I couldn't possibly make the purchase. It was $2,500. How completely ridiculous! Suddenly, nothing made sense. What was I doing? No matter how much money I had, would I ever pay thousands of dollars for a handbag? What was I trying to prove? Who was I trying to be? And yet, after indulging in designer clothing all day long, why stop now? I liked the purse. Why not just buy it?

My capacity for excess had been reached. In a daze, I moved toward the shoe salon, contemplating the purse, frustrated for not buying it, and disgusted for even considering the purchase. Ms. Glamor might have been impressed if privy to the day, but I'd be embarrassed if Grace and Carla knew what I'd been up to.

On the way to the airport, Joan assured me that we could get the last few necessities back in Seattle. Sure enough, a few days later, she whisked me to a waxing appointment for my eyebrows and to Barneys where I slipped my feet into the perfect pair of heels. Mission accomplished. I was a princess for the fall. But what would happen when spring arrived and my coach was a pumpkin again?

It was fun to shop for clothes with Joan and Donna. I liked Prada sandals and looking good, but it sounded depressing to continue spending time tracking down the latest styles in pursuit of the right look. Contrary to what I'd imagined before being able to afford the high prices, I realized a high-fashion wardrobe said more about values and priorities than about wealth. Gucci shoes and Fendi purses might have been Ms. Glamor's dream, but I wasn't a movie star or a socialite and didn't strive to be either. There were more satisfying ways for me to spend my days and take advantage of our fortune. It was time to make a new resolution and start "doing rich my way."

Contemplation & Conversation

- We see glamorous, outrageous images of wealth online, in magazines, and on TV. Have you tried to live up to them? Do you know people who do?

- Have you made purchases or spent money to keep up with friends?

- At one point, Jennifer feels as though wealth can fix every problem. What problems has money fixed in your life? What problems has it created?

Chapter Eleven

ENOUGH

In the early 2000s, with analysts speculating that Amazon was overspending, that the stock was overpriced, and that the company would soon be toast, Amazon's stock price plummeted and our net worth dropped by more than half. But David didn't care. He was too focused on work to be distracted by our personal finances. I didn't care either. After encouraging David to follow his heart and take a job working with books and technology, I was doing my best not to get caught in the unending, unsatisfying pursuit for more, and had made a conscious decision: we had enough. There would always be more, always be less, and there was no magic number. "Enough" was a mindset—one I planned to keep.

Of course, it was relatively easy to feel "enough" when we had more than we needed and life was going well. No longer looking to the images Hollywood was selling, I was enjoying time at the park with Emily and Ali and had signed up for an oil-painting class at a local art school. Believing women need to share their stories, I'd also begun to interview moms, planning to write a book about motherhood. And as I painted in the basement and wrote at my desk, losing myself in my work, I'd begun finding myself again.

But what about David? He left for work at eight o'clock every morning and didn't return until after eight at night—and I missed him. By the time he walked in the door, the girls were asleep, and as we ate dinner, he was miles away, thinking about Amazon's strategy for product expansion and customer loyalty. Then, when the dishes were done, he headed downstairs to do more work in the glow of the computer while I went upstairs to bed alone.

Thinking about how hard David worked, I turned the page in my book without knowing what I'd read. We had all the freedom in the world, what most people imagined as ideal, but I didn't feel the satisfaction that supposedly came with riches. Instead, I felt the importance of having a good relationship with my husband—and again, I missed him.

When he finally dropped into bed, I was still awake.

"Are you okay?" I asked

"What do you mean?"

"You're working nonstop."

"Amazon is growing," he said. "It's a huge challenge."

When David first joined the company, he'd managed the bookstore. Then, with the goal of taking sales to a billion dollars, he'd begun adding music, videos, and toys to Amazon's product line. Once that billion-dollar goal had been achieved and surpassed, he'd started focusing on making Amazon profitable.

"Will you ever slow down . . . or actually leave?" I asked.

Unlike my story of good timing, right place, and a friend on the inside who called about a job at Microsoft, David had done more to earn his success. In high school, he wasn't eating cookies and dreaming of love. He'd spent his time reading and hanging out at RadioShack. After graduating from Princeton, he'd worked in consulting where he showed an aptitude for technology. Then, graduating from Harvard Business School and working at Microsoft, he'd demonstrated a knack for business and leadership. At Amazon, he was excelling yet again. He loved the fast pace and challenge of building a business. But he didn't want to be at Amazon forever. We'd begun to talk about him leaving.

"It's not easy to leave work," he told me. "There's something about working and being a man, providing for my family."

I laughed. "You've already provided."

"Men evaluate themselves, and each other, on their success," he said. "Money is the barometer."

"And you've succeeded astronomically," I said.

In addition to his drive to help Amazon succeed and desire to fulfill his duty as a man, David wanted to be a good son.

"I want my parents to be proud," he said. "I'm worried I'll disappoint them if I don't keep working."

There was no financial reason for him to stay at Amazon, and yet I understood David's drive to succeed. I understood his desire to fulfill his duty as a man as well. At a primal level, I couldn't deny being glad he was a good provider. I too felt an instinctual pull to fulfill my own duty as a wife and mother, to nurture and care for our family. It didn't matter how much money we had or how liberal our views—social norms and gender roles were powerful.

While it was hard to know how we would have reacted if

we'd lost everything or if our roles had been reversed, I would later confirm we weren't the only ones influenced by traditional gender roles. Even as women were making breakthroughs in the workforce, after years of believing men were breadwinners and women homemakers, most people still believe that being a good husband meant being a good provider. In fact, when a woman makes more than her male spouse, both partners can feel uncomfortable, causing women to misreport their incomes, claiming to have earned less than they actually make. Some married career women even opt for less demanding, lower-paying jobs not only to focus on children, but to appear less threatening to their husbands. And in younger married and cohabiting couples, men who depend on a woman's salary have been shown to be five times more likely to cheat than men who earned the same as their partners.

I'd long assumed our family would be like the one I grew up in, with two children spaced two years apart. But Emily and Ali had opened my heart and shifted my thinking. Their presence added new meaning to every experience and was teaching me a new sense of compassion. When Emily showed me a pebble from the playground or Ali started screaming in the cereal aisle, their awe and upset taught me about my own impatience and wonder, helping me find acceptance for both. Sharing parenthood with David brought me joy as well. We were a team, both of us full of love for our daughters, and similarly amazed to be parents—and we both wanted to have a third child.

Talking with another mother from Emily's co-op preschool about how much we were learning from our children and how incredible it was to watch them grow, I was saddened when she told me she wanted another baby but couldn't afford a third child. I was so clueless. Life was unfair. I felt badly for her. I also felt guilty.

Doing my best to be aware and respectful of those around me, I was grateful not to be stuck in the past, confined to the expected. Money clearly made decisions easier, but decisions still had to be made—and the decision to have a third child felt like a huge break from tradition. We were choosing for ourselves, following our hearts. I couldn't imagine a better way of taking advantage of our wealth than becoming a family of five.

In addition to having another baby, as David and I talked about the next chapter in our lives, I felt the world open. Growing up, David had never yearned to be a CEO. He hadn't even anticipated being in the business world. Inspired by his high school French teacher, he had wanted to teach.

"Let's come up with a five-year plan," he suggested. "In the next five years, I'm going to leave Amazon, and find a teaching position. What about you?"

"Let's live abroad," I said.

"I could teach in Paris," David said.

After living in London as a child, going back for a semester my junior year in college, spending another semester in Florence, and working in Tokyo, I felt lucky to have had so much experience abroad. I also knew how much there was to learn from living in another country. A foreign adventure would bring our family closer and give us a new perspective on life.

"Let's make a year somewhere in Europe part of our five-year plan," I said.

Meanwhile, even as we contemplated his departure from Amazon, David was thriving on the challenges and addictive pace, proud of the accomplishments his long hours and smarts helped him achieve. It was exciting to be fully engaged in a job. There was status and bragging rights in being senior vice president. He got a lot out of work. He was making a difference. His job made him happy.

"If I get run over by a bus tomorrow, you'd be the guy in charge," Jeff told David.

"I'm flattered," he replied. "But I wouldn't want to wait around for you to get hit by a bus."

◆ ◆ ◆

When I interviewed people about wealth, it became clear that no specific amount of money brought a sense of enough.

Mary, who had an inheritance as well as a successful career, told me she was primarily working to earn money.

"I'll always work. I'll never have enough," she said. Then, after a few minutes, she added, "I'm not sure my self-esteem is up to not having a job. My identity depends on my position and success. I have a sister-in-law who has never worked, and it's made her insecure. She doesn't know where she fits into the world."

Janet, who had an inheritance and was working for her family foundation, believed she didn't have enough and needed to work.

"I don't need to accumulate more, but it scares me to think of going without a job. I don't like pulling from my resources without adding to them. I can't stop working," she said. Then, considering what she'd just told me, she admitted, "If I'm honest with myself, I know I can, but on a day-to-day basis, that's hard to grasp."

Janet believed it had been important for her to create an identity outside of her family.

"In my twenties, I moved to Guatemala to start a nonprofit. I did my own fundraising and was quite successful," she said. "I was known as a successful nonprofit leader, which gave me confidence. Many inheritors have a hard time separating who they are as individuals from their families and from other people's perceptions."

"The saddest people are inheritors paralyzed by freedom and opportunity," Janet said. "They have no sense of direction, no reason to get out of bed in the morning. There can be a lot of guilt. Money is a magnifying glass. It magnifies what's good, and what's bad. If you're depressed or lost, or if you're happy, then money makes you more so. Poverty can do the same."

After being out of the workforce for years raising her two children, Karen was frustrated when people questioned why she'd decided to get a job.

"It bothers me to have people ask why I went back to work," she said. "The implication is that I don't need the money. Can't I want more money? Can't I enjoy working and find fulfillment and potential in a job? Working makes me feel capable and gives me a way to prove myself."

Karen also believed women needed to talk more about money. She'd worked in finance until her first child was six and noted that men were more direct with each other about how much they were making, openly asking about one another's bonuses.

"Women never ask each other about amounts. But how are we supposed to figure out what's fair when we aren't talking?" Karen said.

Laurie, whose husband had a successful business, told me they had above and beyond the amount they needed.

"But my husband struggles," she said. "He doesn't have enough. He wants to see if he can be even *more* successful."

Working in corporate real estate, Nicole said she didn't think she would ever have enough.

"I like money," she said. "I like it to be mine. My job is my indulgence. It gives me independence. I'm always striving, trying to do better. It's like being in school. I want a good grade. Then, I want a better grade. I enjoy the challenge. There's never enough . . . and I like that feeling of always being out for the next bigger, better prize."

Allison had worked full-time in a science lab and waitressed evenings to support her husband when he quit his job selling cars to focus full-time on a startup. Then, when her husband sold his startup for a lot of money, she found herself wrestling with thoughts about having enough money.

"When I look around at the world, I know we have enough," she said. "But it's easy to get lost in a bubble. We've started going on nicer vacations, remodeling our home, and I feel the need to check myself and keep grounded. Having so much can make you delusional, like there's no way to ever be satisfied."

Allison had recently quit her job, hoping to reduce her stress and get pregnant.

"It took a long time for me to finally leave work, but it has been a good decision," she said. "If I'm not happy and healthy, nothing else matters. But I hate to think of people looking at me as a trophy wife or as not having a brain. Even though my husband and I created our success together, it can feel as though I'm nobody compared to him. When people ask what I do, I always talk about the past because I'm technically not doing anything now."

Sue, whose husband had been part of two successful high-tech startups, was surprised by her response to a market downturn.

"Rationally, I knew we still had a lot, but seeing how much we'd lost, I felt a pit in my stomach," she said. "It's odd to admit. I'm not *really* worried about not having enough. But . . . well . . . maybe a little."

A 2008 study by Boston College's Center on Wealth and Philanthropy entitled "The Joys and Dilemmas of Wealth" confirmed what I was hearing. Even though it didn't make logical sense, the wealthy worried about amounts. The average net worth of the respondents in the study was $78 million, but most claimed to need 25 percent more money than they already possessed. Why was this true? A 2011 article in *The Atlantic*, reporting on the study, suggested that just as our bodies continued to crave cheeseburgers even after we consumed loads of excess fat and sugars, the human mind had yet to evolve to deal with excess money. It seemed the fear of loss also contributed to a desire for more. After all, the way our brains are wired makes the pain of loss twice as intense as the happiness experienced from gain. When asked how much was enough, even John D. Rockefeller, the first American billionaire and richest person in modern history, famously said, "Just a little bit more."

But would "a little bit more" bring happiness? A 2010 Princeton University study showed that happiness plateaued at $75,000 a year. Similarly, a 2016 Case Western University study found each dollar earned had a significant impact in reducing unpleasant feelings for those in the twentieth percentile, but that the emotional benefit of each dollar began to decrease at $70,000, was even lower after $160,000, and disappeared altogether at $200,000. Relationships and social connections, not money, were found to make people the happiest. Generosity was key as well. When given money to spend on themselves or on others, those who spent on others reported feeling happier than those who spent on themselves.

Rather than hoping for "a little bit more," if people at the top gave a set amount to those in lower income brackets, wouldn't we all be happier? Not only would everyone have at least $70,000 a year, those of us sharing our resources would benefit from the positive feeling of helping others, and we'd all get to live in a more equal, just, and socially connected society.

◆　◆　◆

In July 2001, staring down at a pregnancy test, I watched a second pink line slowly appear. We were going to have another baby!

Over the weeks that followed, my excitement grew, but nausea had me crawling into bed.

"Are you sleeping?" Emily asked.

"No. But I don't feel good," I admitted. "I'm resting."

Believing Emily had already heard the news, I told her about the baby. As the words settled in, she smiled. We then had our first conversation about how to care for an infant.

"Can I hold the baby?" Emily asked.

"Of course."

"Like what? Like this?" she asked, sitting down on the floor and putting an imaginary baby on her lap. "Can I use the rocking chair?"

"You're such a good big sister," I said. "Will you help me feed the baby?"

"With a bottle?"

Emily and I talked about bottles and what babies like best until Ali padded into the bedroom and crawled onto the bed. She didn't ask what we were talking about. She'd likely heard about the baby too and didn't need to know more. We already had a baby. That baby was her.

"Read to me," she said. "Please."

On the morning of September 11, 2001, there were hurried footsteps on the stairs and David rushed into our bedroom, telling me an airplane had crashed into the Twin Towers in New York City. It was hard to comprehend. Together, we watched the smoke rising from the buildings, our hearts going out to New York as we learned about the attack. Later that morning, sickened by the devastation, but feeling well enough to get out of bed, I spent a couple of hours with Carla and Grace. While the three of us were talking about what was going on in New York, Carla suddenly looked over at me and asked if I was okay.

"I feel strange," I said. "I'm worried about the baby."

Later that day, I sat in my doctor's waiting room in front of a tank of tropical fish and watched other pregnant women come and go. My regular doctor wasn't in, but someone else from her practice had agreed to see me.

"Let's take a listen," he said, showing me into his office.

He gave me a reassuring smile and got out the heart rate monitor. Moving the probe in circles along my stomach, he grew increasingly serious. After a few minutes, he looked up.

"Let's do an ultrasound."

He pulled the machine over and began probing again while I looked over my shoulder at the monitor, watching the black and white images swirl around on the screen until a tiny figure swung into view. It looked like a gummy bear with two short arms and two little legs. There was no heartbeat.

"No!" I yelled.

Bursting into tears, I turned toward the wall, trying to go back in time. Back to when my baby had a bright shiny pulse, when I was sick, and Emily and Ali were going to be big sisters. It was just seconds ago. In a sudden panic, with a sense of desperation, longing for a different outcome, I screamed out again. I wanted to take another look at the monitor, just to make sure, but afraid of further confirmation, I stared at the wall in the opposite direction, sobbing and wishing my husband were with me, the motionless image fixed in my head.

At home, I lay on the sofa, David by my side. He didn't know what to say. I was silent too. And when Emily asked what was wrong and we told her as gently as possible that we weren't going to have a baby, she clapped her hands to her ears.

"Stop. Don't say it," she said, hiding her face in the pillows on the sofa.

Trying to make sense of the miscarriage for Emily, I spoke of life's natural rhythm, of flowers, and of returning to the earth. But it was hard to understand the loss for myself. David stayed home the next morning, offering much-needed support. Hearing from neighbors and parents from the girls' school brought me comfort. It was helpful to learn miscarriage was more common than I'd realized. With people sharing their experiences and telling me their stories, I felt more connected to those around me. A new sense of enough began to bloom, one that wasn't just a mindset or conscious decision, and had nothing to do with money.

Contemplation & Conversation

- Do you think your gender influences how you view money? Is your self-worth and identity linked to the amount of money you have?

- Do you have enough money? Is there a magic amount that would *feel* like enough? How would you *know* you had enough? Does your partner share you views?

- How does it make you feel to hear that people with $78 million believe they need 25 percent more? Could you imagine yourself in the same position? Of the people Jennifer interviewed, is there one you relate to most?

- Jennifer believes we would all be happier if we lived in a more equal, just, and socially connected society. Do you agree?

Chapter Twelve

DOWN-TO-EARTH

When David and I first traveled together, we put the car in long-term parking and took a shuttle to the airport. Not long after that, when Emily entered our lives, we allowed ourselves the indulgence of parking at the terminal. Then, with Ali's birth, more accustomed to our resources and willing to use them, we began hiring a town car and a driver named Boris. Although he didn't wear white gloves or a black cap like the chauffeurs in old movies, Boris preferred to be seen and not heard. Picking us up at our house and dropping us at the curb outside check-in, he maintained a relationship with me that was nothing like the one I shared with Noreen, our housekeeper, or with May, our nanny—and it was surprisingly nice to simply be served. But was being driven by Boris a problem for the girls? They hadn't experienced anything else.

One afternoon, when we were on our way to the airport, Boris driving, David in the front, and me between Emily and Ali in the back, Emily asked if we were late.

"We could have left a little earlier," I said. "But we're fine."

"Will the plane wait for us?"

My eyes dropped to the pink princess backpack on her lap.

Emily was not an inexperienced traveler. She knew how planes and flights worked.

"What do you mean?" I said, staring at the back of Boris' head.

"You know," she said. "Will it be one of those small planes just for our family?"

"No," I said. "This one won't wait."

"Is it a lie-down plane?" Ali asked. "Will the seats turn into beds?"

My head swiveled around to look at our younger daughter, snuggled into the plush leather of the town car as we glided down the highway toward the airport for our flight to Hawaii. She looked innocent enough. But imagining her with a pink feather boa, whipping out her wand, turning princes into frogs and squash into flying saucers, I was concerned. Both girls had traveled more often and in more luxury than most people did in a lifetime. With our six-year-old wondering if we were taking a private jet and our four-year-old questioning whether we were flying international first class, I believed something had to change.

"What have we done?" I muttered to David as we helped Boris unload the trunk. "And what are we going to do?"

"I'm not sure," he admitted.

It was fun to drive up to the plane and see a good-looking man in a uniform at the top of the stairs, but the excess and indulgence of flying private made me worry about the girls. What attitude would they adopt? How would they view their future and the world around them? Emily and Ali were already living in a small corner of the world. It didn't seem wise to push their experience even further away from what most people knew. We could tell them flying alone was rare and special, that not many people could even consider such a thing. But if we continued to fly alone as a family, would they truly understand? Private jets would seem like just another normal part of their lives. So, while David's fascination with planes had him chartering another jet for a weekend with friends, I put private jet travel into the same category as a high-fashion wardrobe. I didn't want either in our life.

The irony of giving up private jets to keep Emily and Ali grounded in the wider, wilder world was not completely lost on me. Private jets simply seemed like an obvious and relatively easy place to draw a line. For their sanity and awareness of normal life, I wanted Emily and Ali to experience getting to the airport on time, going through security, and waiting in line with everyone else. I wanted the same for myself. Or at least, I wanted a sense of understanding and connection that came from being with other people. It felt important to be in touch with the experiences most people knew. But as I shunned private jets, declaring them overly indulgent and excessive, I fully intended to continue flying first-class—and the hypocrisy was not completely lost on me either. Neither was the fact that we were highly advantaged to be flying in the first place.

A decade later, when Emily and Ali were away at college, my relationship with private jets would change yet again. Flying private still felt excessive, but with David and me alone in our nest, no watchful eyes upon us, I enjoyed the ease and efficiency. We hired a plane to get from San Francisco to New Jersey for David's twenty-fifth college reunion. Later the same year, I flew eight friends from Napa to Tucson for a girls' tennis weekend. And when a friend asked me to join her and a group of women for a hiking trip in Patagonia, one of them flew the six of us from Oakland to El Calafate on her company's corporate jet. But as David signed up for NetJets, I was still glad we had stopped flying private when our daughters were younger.

When talking about wealth, some people I interviewed mentioned private planes quietly under their breath as though testing my reaction before sharing their experiences.

"My husband loves his toys," Betsy finally said. "He owns a quarter of a plane."

"Do friends know?" I asked.

"No!" she said, her eyes growing large. "No one has any idea. I want to be sensitive to other people and not make it a big deal."

Betsy then told me about taking a couple of family members on the plane from San Francisco to Washington, D.C. in January 2017 for the Women's March.

"I told them it was a once-in-a-lifetime thing," she said.

Julie, who spent years trying to hide her wealth, found it easiest and most comfortable to think about money as a way to buy time. When her oldest was starting high school, her family began flying private, and she justified the decision as a time-saving move.

"At first, the kids were amazed. They thought it was so cool," Julie said. "Now the older ones tell me they're worried about our youngest. They say he doesn't know any different and needs to fly coach."

Laurie laughed as she imagined the rude awaking her children would have when they were out of the house and living on their own.

"I never flew first class, not until I was in my thirties and had saved enough miles to upgrade," she said. "But our kids have only flown first or private. When they're in their thirties, they're going to take a huge step backward."

Back when I was rejecting private planes, when Emily was six and Ali four, Kim, a friend and fellow UCDS parent, asked if I wanted to carpool. At first, I said, "No." It was easier to let May, our nanny, do the driving. But then, hoping to be more connected with other mothers, and more involved in the school community, I gave carpooling a try—and as soon as I became Emily's chauffeur, I realized just how much I'd been missing. Picking up Emily and her friend and taking them to ballet class, I got to listen to the two of them chattering and giggling in the back. They had so much to say. Once they started laughing, neither could stop, which made me laugh too.

After a few weeks of taking my turn driving, in addition to enjoying the conversations, I felt a growing closeness to Kim. When I dropped off her daughter, the two of us spent time talking in the driveway, discussing a problem we had with another parent at school or telling one another about a recipe we liked. We started depending on one another in other ways too. When I was running late and needed someone to pick up Ali and Emily, instead of immediately calling May, I turned to Kim. It made me happy to have her request my help too, asking me to let a repairman into her house when she couldn't get home in time. What's more, as our lives intertwined, Emily got to know and trust another mother, giving me the sense of being part of a village. So, when another mother from UCDS suggested a swap, asking if Ali could spend Tuesday afternoons at her house and her daughter could spend Thursday afternoons at ours, I jumped at the opportunity.

"It's isolating to hire help," I said to a friend whose husband worked at Microsoft. "Relying on our nanny, I was missing out on what so many mothers share."

"Maybe," she said. "But it's easier to just pay someone."

It was easy. May was a huge support. So was Noreen. Boris too. A lot of independence was gained from hiring help. It was a luxury to have other people do everyday tasks I didn't want to do myself. But there was a downside. Paying someone else to do what other mothers did for each other kept me on the outside, disconnected. I missed out on the community and closeness that developed when neighbors and fellow parents shared chores, complaints, and advice, in touch and in tune with one another's lives.

"She has a pool inside her house," Emily said one afternoon when I picked her up from a playdate.

"Sounds nice," I said, looking at my daughter in the rearview mirror.

"She has an elevator inside her house too," Emily said. "It's glass. I wish we had an elevator."

"We don't need an elevator."

"They have a trampoline room," Emily said.

When my mother had picked me up from an overnight decades earlier, she'd been uncomfortable with the wealth of my friend's family and hadn't liked hearing me talk about their fancy living room and private club. With Emily excited about elevators and indoor pools, I too was uncomfortable. But I wasn't envious or worried about keeping up. I wasn't concerned about Emily being too interested in money either. Not only had I joined the socioeconomic class my mother never much liked, I'd vaulted into a strangely disconnected, unfairly advantaged stratosphere, living in territory I hadn't known existed. I could join the after-school shuffle and wrangle kids into our car, doing my best to be connected and involved, but I wasn't grounded in the reality most people knew. How would Emily and Ali be down-to-earth? Driving carpool and avoiding private jets didn't seem like enough.

With money an off-limits subject, not something other parents discussed, David and I turned to Charles, our financial advisor, looking to him as confidant and friend. He knew our financial situation, and with him, money was an acceptable conversation topic.

"We're concerned about Emily and Ali," I told him. "They're living in such a bubble."

Charles reassured us Emily and Ali were fine.

"You won't have the same issues as some of my other newly wealthy clients," he said. "One guy has built a huge wine cellar and is collecting expensive bottles of wine. He's teaching his kids to spend and won't have anything left to give them. He's on a trajectory to go broke in five years."

As Charles told us that creating a trust fund for each of our daughters was an obvious and necessary building block for a solid estate plan, I thought he was missing the point. Trust fund kids had been on the periphery of my life during college and seemed strange and unknowable. I wanted the girls to be aware of their advantages, respectful of others, and in touch with the world around them.

"It's a good idea to give them some money when they are relatively young, like twenty-five," Charles told us. "That way, they can blow it all and get another chance five years later."

I looked at David as Charles continued.

"From my experience, even if money has been part of their lives all along, kids don't know how to handle large sums."

"I guess it will depend on who they grow up to be," I said. "They're two different people. What ends up being right for one might not be right for the other."

"Statistically, it's your kids' kids who will have the problems," Charles said.

After growing up middle-class, working part-time jobs, and making financial trade-offs, David and I were still somewhat connected to normal life. Our understanding of reality was a benefit to Emily and Ali. When that same connection to regular life was a generation removed, children often failed to have the same values and work ethic that built the wealth in the first place. The third generation was notorious for losing everything. In fact, the phenomenon was described in proverbs such as, "Shirtsleeves to shirtsleeves in three generations." In Lancaster, England, where workmen wore heavy-soled shoes people said, "Clogs to clogs in three generations." In Japan, the saying was, "Rice paddies to rice paddies in three generations." And the Scottish proverb was, "The father buys, the son builds, the grandchild sells, and his son begs."

Once, in a writing group, when a British woman asked if we were raising our daughters to work, I didn't understand her question. How could you raise kids not to work? But she'd never been expected to get a job. Instead, she'd been taught to value education, artistic pursuits, and philanthropy. While I realized there were many kinds of valid, happy lives, there was still no question in my mind that Emily and Ali needed to get jobs. David felt the same. Work was central to the way people lived. Not only did a job provide financial, psychological, and emotional independence, a job offered a sense of purpose, structure, and a way to connect and contribute to society. As Joseph Conrad suggested, work could help the girls know themselves better too—and was still something I missed. But how would they be motivated and driven if there was no financial reason for them to earn a paycheck? Would wealth dampen their sense of ambition? Would it hurt their sense of satisfaction and fulfillment? What about their ability to connect with friends?

Thankfully, in addition to talking to Charles, I could talk to Donna and Lynn. After being co-workers at Microsoft, we'd seen one another through courtship, marriage, and the birth of our first and second children. We were also classmates in the school of new wealth and shared an understanding, our mutual good fortune part of our bond, giving me a sense of community, especially when it wasn't possible to talk with other people. No one wanted to hear about issues they wished they had, or about problems that sounded inconsequential. Donna and Lynn understood and shared my concerns, and I was grateful the three of us had gone through so much together.

Later, Julie would tell me how thankful she was to have experienced new wealth with a group of other women.

"There were several of us all going through the same thing together," she said. "It was so nice not to be alone."

Over time, even though she didn't handle her money the same way her friends handled theirs, she continued to be thankful for their presence in her life.

"Most of them think I'm crazy," she said. "They're into jewelry and handbags and wonder why I'm not more decked out. But those women mean a lot to me. We've gone through something significant together, which has made us quite close."

My experience with Donna and Lynn was similar. When it came to money and our children, I was happy we could share ideas.

"Are you worried about how money is affecting your kids?" I asked them.

"Not really," Donna said. "But everyone else seems to. My sister is always asking why we don't buy our kids more stuff and friends want to know what we're doing to keep them from being spoiled."

"People are hoping to see a train wreck," Lynn said. "They're imagining themselves in the same position, wondering what they'd do, probably thinking they'd handle things better."

"Will you give money to your kids?" I asked Lynn.

"No way. They need to work," she said.

"Aren't you worried they'll be resentful?" I asked.

"It's our money, not theirs," Donna said.

"Your financial situation could be a real benefit to them," I said. "Why not let them follow their dreams?"

"What will motivate them to get started?" Lynn asked. "How will they start dreaming in the first place?"

"There are plenty of motivators. Maybe they'll feel a call to create or help others. Or they'll want to work in an animal shelter," I said.

"You're too idealistic," Lynn said with a snort. "Money is the best way to motivate people. It's the way society works. We need to eat. We need shelter. Then we want some jewelry."

"But money isn't the only motivator," Donna said. "People work for many reasons." Turning to me, she said, "Lynn knows fear is very motivating."

The three of us laughed. Lynn had no obvious reason for concern, but she'd long been worried about ending up shoeless on the street, which was one of the reasons she was continuing to work, keeping her skills up to date, and ensuring she would always be employable.

"I want our kids to see me getting up every day and going to the office," Lynn said. "My dad worked three jobs when I was growing up."

"Kids learn from what's going on around them," Donna said.

Donna then told us that her children had recently drawn a picture for Matt to hang in his office.

"They made me a picture too," she said. "I was supposed to 'take it with me to the stores.' Can you believe it? Do my children think all I do is shop? That's not the behavior I want to be modeling."

I laughed. But I wouldn't be laughing as loudly a couple of years later when Ali wrote a Mother's Day poem about a mother who spent too much time at her computer and not enough time with her daughter.

When friends told me, "Your daughters are so nice," or "Your kids are so grounded," I heard these comments as code for surprise that rich kids could be pleasant, not obnoxious. Given the expectations and preconceptions around wealth, it seemed Emily and Ali would need to work extra hard and be extra nice to prove themselves likable and competent. People would likely link their achievements and failures to money too—for good reason. Wealth gave our daughters many advantages. They were set up to succeed. Growing up in a stable home, they were already well ahead of kids whose basic needs were not being met. And with access to education, healthcare, and social connections, they were way more privileged than most. But wealth could cause problems too, distorting their view of the world and paralyzing them with too much freedom and too many choices.

When Ali was in third grade and the two of us were walking home from school together, she told me that kindergarteners looked small.

"When I was in kindergarten," she said. "I thought I was bigger than that."

"Now that you're in third grade, you *are* bigger," I said.

"When I'm in fifth grade, like Emily, will third graders look small?"

"Probably."

"When I'm in middle school, the kids in elementary school will look small. When I'm in high school, the middle school kids will look small. Then I'll go to college. Then I'll go to work. Then I'll stop working."

"Most people don't stop working," I said. "Most people work until they are Grandma's and Grandpa's age."

Thinking about Ali's view of the future, hoping to teach her the value of money, David and I started giving the girls an allowance, doling out a weekly dollar fifty to Emily and a dollar to Ali. We assembled cardboard piggybanks from Charles, our financial advisor, encouraging them to put their money aside for saving, spending, and giving.

At first, allowance was a hit and we felt successful. But after several months, once the novelty had worn off, we forgot to give the girls their money. Since Emily and Ali forgot about allowance too, weeks passed without any cash exchanging hands. Then, when we were out and Emily or Ali asked for some candy and we told them to use their allowance, they said we owed them, asked to borrow, and it was clear no lessons were being taught or learned. Even when we tried a monthly schedule, telling Emily and Ali they needed to ask for their allowance at the beginning of each month, we didn't have success. But I wasn't worried.

Allowance didn't seem as critical as making sure our daughters felt loved. I also wanted them to be integral, contributing members of our family, which meant having dinner together. Not only were meals a good time to connect and share stories from the day, everyone could participate. I cooked, while Emily and Ali set the table. Then, after eating, the girls cleared the table, and David did the dishes. The girls had other responsibilities too, like making their beds and keeping their room tidy. But it could be difficult to enforce the rules. One afternoon, when Ali called out, asking if Noreen was coming tomorrow, I found her sitting on the floor of her bedroom in a sea of tiny white papers. It was tempting to let Noreen make the mess disappear the next day, but I told Ali she needed to clean up when she was done.

It seemed important that the girls take responsibility for their messes and for us to eat together every night but I believed the best way to ensure Emily and Ali were grounded was to exhibit the behavior and attitude I wanted to see from them. They knew that we viewed affluence as a tool and a benefit, not something to flaunt or a source of pride. They witnessed us making trade-offs, compromises, and not buying whatever we wanted. We enjoyed meals at nice restaurants and traveled abroad, but we saved dinner leftovers for lunch the next day and were appreciative of our ability to travel as a family. They also observed David working nonstop and saw my involvement at their school.

By the time Emily and Ali were in high school, they were both working hard and succeeding academically. Emily had dedicated herself to a sport she loved for a decade. Ali had a job in a clothing store where she worked after school and on weekends throughout her junior and senior years of high school. But I continued to worry, unsure how our wealth was affecting their lives—and my concern was shared.

"When I was in high school, I felt the pressure of necessity," Sue told me. "I needed to get a job and knew I'd have to work for a living. That knowledge and need shaped who I am. Our boys don't feel that same pressure. It's hard to know who they'll become without that same need to work."

"We're not planning to give the kids any money," Nicole said. "They'll get money when we die, but not before. They need to work."

When Nicole's oldest went to college and she told him how much she was giving him as an allowance, he complained, saying he was accustomed to a certain lifestyle and needed more.

"I told him he'd have to work if he wanted the same lifestyle," Nicole said. "If he needed money, he'd have to make it himself . . . and he got a job as a deejay."

Betsy, who described herself as the "family CFO," made a point to teach her three children how to manage their money. Early on, she helped them set up checking accounts, gave them a monthly allowance, and taught them the importance of living within a budget. But with one of her children in the workforce, another in college, and the youngest at boarding school, she was concerned.

"We've been giving the two at school quarterly allowances," she said. "But they keep running out of money. We're paying room and board, but they're constantly having food delivered, going out to eat, and using up their allowance."

Over spring break, when her college-aged son went on a trip with a friend, and called her from the road, asking for money, Betsy wanted to tell him he needed to figure things out. But her husband, who had grown up never having enough, didn't want his son to go without, especially when he didn't have to.

"It's a problem. I'm not sure what to do," she said. "My husband and I try to set limits, but the limits are artificial—and our kids know it."

Her oldest wanted to live off campus for his final year of college, so Betsy told him he first had to successfully live on campus without overspending.

"An off-campus apartment has become my carrot," she said.

Meanwhile, her twenty-three-year-old son had a job but wasn't making enough to cover the cost of rent and had asked to move back home "for a month," which turned into two, then three, then longer. Neither Betsy nor her son was happy with the arrangement.

"I've begun charging him rent but it's backfiring," she said. "He owes me money. But he knows the situation is contrived. What am I going to do? Kick him out?"

Loren, who had grown up in poverty, was frustrated by her boyfriend's older children, who seemed ungrateful for their advantages.

"After growing up with nothing and seeing all they have, it's hard not to feel resentful, even jealous," she said. "They can be so rude and careless. When I cook for them, I have to make them thank me."

Julie's oldest son was about to start college.

"I'm not sure what to give him for an allowance," she said. "He wants us to 'throw him to the wolves' so he can learn to fend for himself."

Julie and her husband were considering giving him a large lump sum, encouraging him to invest, and telling him he had to live on the money for the next four years.

"The experience of managing money on his own would be good for him," Julie said. "He needs to understand how finances work before he turns twenty-five and gets a lot more."

Laurie, who had three children in middle school, wasn't particularly concerned about them being spoiled. She attributed their good attitude and awareness to the closeness of their family and to each of her children having jobs. Her oldest worked at the business her husband started, her daughter babysat, and all three did chores around the house.

"But I'm always questioning our decisions," she said. "For example, I wasn't sure what to do when the kids outgrew their bikes. My husband wanted to just buy three new ones, but it seemed like we should wait until Christmas or a birthday. Finally, I accepted that we didn't need to make it a special purchase. We just got the bikes so we could ride together as a family. But I'm concerned we're setting them up for a shock in the future."

Janet, an heiress, did her best to keep her money a secret when she was in college and in her early twenties.

"I flew under the radar a lot," she said. "When I first started working for our family foundation, I learned to say I worked for 'a' family foundation. I wanted to be transparent but didn't want to open that whole side of myself up when meeting someone for the first time. It made dating hard."

After spending a lot of time in Guatemala, where she'd started a nonprofit, Janet found it difficult to transition to and from Manhattan.

"When I'm working with indigenous people, I can become numb to the poverty. A child begging starts to seem normal— and that bothers me," she said. "It bothers me how quickly I become numb to wealth too. Back in New York, living in a multimillion-dollar apartment, surrounded by people who fly in jets, I hear myself saying, 'I'm not *that* rich.' But compared to who? It's hard to feel grounded, to remember this is not how most people live. I try to focus on the good we are trying to do with philanthropy. I try to spend a lot of time in Guatemala too."

Karen's ex-husband lavished their two children with expensive gifts and money.

"When they were younger, the kids wanted to vacation with their father, not me," Karen said. "I liked going on more educational trips, and he'd fly around in a private jet and take them to extravagant resorts."

When their daughter needed a car and Karen was thinking about getting her a Chevy, her ex-husband bought her a Range Rover.

"She didn't want it," Karen said. "But he told her she didn't have a right to an opinion if he was paying."

Soon afterward, Karen's daughter decided not to take any more money from her father. She sold the Range Rover and sent him the cash.

"When she was no longer dependent on him, she accidentally used one of his old credit cards for a medical appointment," Karen said. "He called her immediately, saying he noticed she was taking his money."

Meanwhile, Karen's son was thrilled when he could drive his father's Tesla.

"He drove up wearing sunglasses, moccasins, and driving gloves," Karen said, looking skyward. "He's now about to start a job in finance, just like his dad. He's going to be making a lot of money. I'm a bit worried about him. I'm worried about my daughter too. Given her interests, she won't ever make much."

Experts recommend talking to children about money when they are young, but just as David and I weren't good with allowance, we never felt the timing was right. Conversations about money hadn't been part of our own childhoods and it was difficult to know how to bring up the subject. We had no idea what to say or how Emily and Ali would react. There were so many potential pitfalls. What's more, with them in school, going to class, involved in sports and activities, and spending time with friends, the details of our financial situation didn't seem relevant to their lives. They were just kids. They were lucky money wasn't a worry or something they needed to think about. So, although we did our best to make sure Emily and Ali knew they were lucky, we fell back on what we'd learned growing up and allowed the specifics of our finances to disappear.

A 2017 *New York Times* article titled, "How the Wealthy Talk to Their Children" confirmed that wealth was difficult to discuss, even within families. According to the article, "Two-thirds of the [fifty-seven] people polled by Wilmington Trust . . . said they were, 'apprehensive about sharing inheritance details.'" Only one in ten had fully disclosed amounts to their children. Wealth advisors acknowledged that families who'd lived with wealth over generations had an advantage over people like David and me, who had no system in place to serve as a guide—all of which was a relief to hear. Many other parents felt the way we did.

When the girls were twenty and eighteen, Emily a junior in college and Ali about to start her freshman year, we agreed it was time to talk to them about money. But we still didn't know how to broach the subject or how much to divulge. Even good news could be difficult to digest. Emily and Ali were doing well, happily hiking along, aiming for the summit, facing setbacks, making progress, and sharing their joys and fears with their friends. Telling them about the money they had would be like giving them a pair of magic shoes. Those shoes could get them to the top of the mountain in half the time and with less effort, but would they feel overwhelmed, their goals called into question, their future uncertain? Would they want to keep those shoes a secret, pleased about the security, but wary of being singled out, their friends looking at them differently? We believed Emily and Ali needed to know about their wealth and wanted them to see it as a benefit. But money represented obligation and responsibility. The doubts and dilemmas were real too.

Before talking to our daughters, curious what other parents in our situation were doing and had done, we decided to ask—and there was clearly a lot of pent-up energy around the topic of children and wealth. As soon as David sent an email to a couple of friends, suggesting we get together for dinner to discuss giving money to our children, the responses were immediate. And when we met, conversation was animated. None of us had ever discussed wealth in such detail with other people.

Our first dinner was with John and Claire, an Amazon executive and his wife. John had grown up middle-class and had been extremely successful at Amazon. Early on, he and his wife had set up college plans and trusts for their two children. Then, when each of their children turned seventeen, John and Clair had them meet with their financial advisor.

"We wanted our kids to understand how their college education was being paid for," John explained. "It was a good way for the kids to get to know our family advisor."

Later, John and Claire told their children about their trusts. "The money is theirs," John said. "They have complete freedom to use it any way they want. We wrote them each a formal letter explaining that the money had been invested to provide for their health, maintenance, education, and support."

Without divulging the total amount, the letter also explained that their children could expect to receive a lump sum every year with larger sums at age twenty-three and twenty-five, half of the remaining value of the trust at thirty, and the balance at forty.

"We had each of them meet with our financial advisor alone, so they could ask questions without trying to please us or meet our expectations," John said. "We want them to see this as a gift that helps them feel secure and gives them choices."

We next spoke with our good friends, Donna and Matt who had set up trusts for each of their three children, the oldest of whom was a junior in college.

"We're not sure what to tell our kids," Matt admitted.

Donna was concerned about the decisions their children might make and didn't think any of them were ready to get a large sum of money.

"It's more our money than theirs," she said. "I want to guide them as they make choices."

The four of us agreed that information about money needed to be doled out slowly. Too much too soon seemed problematic.

"I think they'll need prenuptial agreements," Donna said.

"I completely agree," I said.

If things went wrong, at a time of emotional turmoil, I wanted our daughters to be protected from financial loss. More than that, it was important that Emily and Ali discussed money with their partners and had ongoing conversations about finances. Having a shared understanding about money was not only critical to any union, talking created trust and built intimacy. There was nothing romantic about taking out the garbage or doing the dishes, but just as couples needed to negotiate those tasks, conversations and agreements about how money was spent, saved, and divided were essential too.

After talking with Matt and Donna, we enjoyed dinner with Joe and Ann. Joe, an ex-Microsoft manager had grown up lower middle-class, became an engineer, joined Microsoft, and had done extremely well. His wife, Ann, hadn't worked in years, and their three adult children were all in the workforce, two with families of their own. Joe and Ann hadn't set up trusts but had always supported their children financially.

"For a long time, Ann and I talked about tailoring gifts to each of the kids," Joe said. "But in the end, it didn't make sense."

When their oldest was about to buy a house, they gave all three children the same large amount, explaining that the money was intended for housing. One of their children ended up buying a big home, another purchased a smaller place and put money in the bank, and the third hadn't yet settled down.

"They know we're here for them, but they don't expect us to give them money," Joe said. "They don't need it either."

After hearing directly from other couples, talking to the girls about their trusts didn't feel as overwhelming, and our next dinner conversation was with Emily and Ali during a family vacation. We let them know ahead of time that we wanted to talk about finances, and after being shown into a recommended restaurant, down a narrow staircase to a small room surrounded floor-to-ceiling with bottles of red wine, we ordered drinks, bruschetta, artichokes, and burrata, and Emily asked what exactly we wanted to discuss.

To begin, we reiterated that we were fortunate to be on vacation, together as a family. We talked about being lucky, about the choices we'd made, and the benefits of education. David then explained how we were paying for college.

"When you were little, we set up funds specifically for education," he said. "The money we invested will cover the cost of college and probably graduate school too, if you want to go."

"What if we don't want to go to graduate school?" Ali asked.

"You don't have to go," I said.

"What happens to the money if we don't?" Emily asked.

"I'm not sure," I said. "But it's there if you need it."

"It needs to be used for education," David said. "If you don't use it, we could probably give it to one of your cousins."

We then explained that we'd invested additional money in trusts for each of them, that the investments were doing well, and that they would get large sums of money in the not-so-distant future. Then, hoping to help them get more accustomed to handling cash, we told them we were going to give allowance another try.

"We'll have money deposited into your accounts every month," David said. "It's to buy things for yourself, to take your friends out. It's to spend, not save."

Starting in middle school, influenced by her two best friends—and by us—Ali had become very careful with her spending. Even after working for two years in high school to earn money of her own, she didn't spend much.

"I know it can be hard to spend money on things when your

friends can't," I said. "You don't want to make people uncomfortable. But I bet your friends would appreciate you taking them out to lunch."

"It's too awkward," Ali said. "I don't want to show off. It would be embarrassing."

"It's lucky I have Hannah as a friend," Emily said, referring to a college buddy who was from a wealthy family. "She has no issue with being rich. She spends a lot of money and she's super generous with everyone. It makes it easier for me to spend and be generous too."

"Sometimes, when a bunch of us get coffee, one of my friends says she can't join us, that she doesn't want to spend the money," Ali said. "But she clearly has enough. I don't want to be like that, using money as an excuse or pretending not to have it when I do."

"You can't hide what you have or cover up how much our family has because you're embarrassed or want people to like you," Emily said. "It's annoying. People know and it's irritating when people pretend."

"Yeah, I know," Ali said.

"Some of my friends can't afford to go out," Emily continued. "They're so appreciative when I buy drinks or pay for dinner. It feels good. I've never had a bad experience. I'd rather be overly generous than not go out because a friend can't afford to."

It was a relief to hear Emily and Ali talk. They had each other. They seemed to have a relatively grounded view of money too. If anything, I wished they would spend more freely. It was hard to know how wealth would influence their choices and decisions in the future, but in the present, they seemed to be enjoying the advantage of not having to think much about finances at all.

Contemplation & Conversation

- Do you give your children an allowance? What have they learned from having their own money?

- What do you think motivates people? What can lead to apathy? Does motivation come from nature or nurture? What role does money play in motivation?

- What is your biggest concern about money and your children? What attitudes and actions do you hope they adopt?

- What are your thoughts about prenuptial agreements? Would you want your children to have a prenuptial agreement or would it upset you if they did?

Chapter Thirteen

GIVING

W hen I was a kid and stopped to stare at a man playing guitar on the street, mesmerized by his singing and the shiny coins in his guitar case, my parents urged me to keep walking, telling me we didn't give to beggars.

"That guy probably makes a good living," my father said to my mother. "I bet he dresses in old clothes to get more."

During my childhood, my mother and I took bags of clothes to Goodwill, donated canned peaches to food drives, and talked about the importance of helping the needy. But I never saw my parents giving money away. With my father worried about bills and my mother fearful of spending, there never seemed to be anything extra to give. I also got the sense that charity was for chumps, that people asking for money were out to take advantage of people like us who worked hard and paid taxes.

"We've been saving, so we have to pay full college tuition," I heard my father complaining to my mother. "Other people cheat the system. They have nothing in the bank, but have big houses and expensive cars—and get financial aid."

Just as it took time for my thinking about saving and spending to change, my understanding of giving and charity took time to grow and evolve—longer than I might have expected, and longer than I might have hoped. When I first joined Microsoft, it wasn't my good salary or stock options that prompted me to give. It was the people around me. Only after witnessing co-workers donating to local causes did I even think to do the same. Then, inspired, I signed up to donate a small percent of my paycheck to United Way and sent a $1,000 check to Planned Parenthood for the good work they were doing.

Similarly, when I first joined the board at Emily's daycare, giving wasn't top-of-mind. But during a board meeting, as we grappled with how to increase employee pay, talking about raising tuition, expanding the facility, and cutting back on staff, my heart began to pound. It suddenly dawned on me I could do something to help. As soon as that meeting was over, I drove directly to the bank and withdrew thousands in cash. It was exciting to think of giving gifts to all the caregivers and staff. But uninterested in being seen as somebody rich, I made the donations in secret, sneaking into the daycare at night and putting envelopes with $200 into each of the fifteen mailboxes.

Not long after giving anonymously at the daycare, I met with one of the caregivers for coffee and watched as she put a five-dollar bill into the tip jar.

"That's nice," I said.

"What?"

"Giving such a big tip."

"It's nothing," she said. "They work hard."

"You work hard too. Do you really have an extra five dollars to give away?"

"I don't like having too much money," she said. "It makes me uncomfortable. It's the way I live. When I have money, I spend it. Or I give it away."

She then shared a story from when she was ten years old and found a wad of bills on the street. She'd taken the money into a nearby store, and when the guy at the counter told her to keep it, she didn't know what to do.

"It must have been sixty bucks," she said. "I took it home. But I got rid of it somehow. I don't feel good when I have too much. I don't want to be like rich people."

Breezing past her comment about the rich, drawn to her lack of attachment to money, I felt compelled to be more generous. Soon afterward, hoping to ensure other women benefited from the support and camaraderie I'd experienced in my PEPS group, I gave the largest amount I'd ever given, writing a $5,000 check to the PEPS organization. Then, after years of listening to public radio, David and I gave $10,000 to NPR, proud to be stepping up and giving to an organization that was an important part of our lives. We then attended our first UCDS auction.

Parents, teachers, and staff had dressed for the occasion, many in elegant evening wear and sparkling jewels. The event space was elaborately decorated too. Colorful DNA chains dangled from the ceiling and bent wires and beads were nestled into centerpieces, reminders of the school's goal to raise funds for a new science lab.

For the first hour, David and I talked with other parents and surveyed the silent auction items. We then sat down at our table with friends and I began searching through the centerpiece for Emily's artwork.

"I think they're supposed to be atoms," someone said. "Is that Emily's?"

I held up a colorful jumble of beads and peered around the table, silently assessing the other creations, believing Emily's just might be the best. Our children's art was meant to tug at our hearts and provoke generosity. There was also competition in the air.

The mesclun salads arrived and the head of school took the microphone at the front of the room, welcoming us to the evening and encouraging us to give. She then asked us to raise our paddles for teacher enrichment and financial aid, and as the auctioneer called for $5,000 gifts, David held our number high.

The salad plates were cleared, the chicken and salmon entrees arrived, and we gossiped about the items to be auctioned off during dessert.

"Did you see what the Boylston family donated?" someone asked. "Time at their Palm Springs home, including flights and a chef for the weekend. I bet their place is beautiful."

"Yeah, but what's up with the Williams? It's not like they couldn't afford to buy several restaurants. They only gave a dinner for two."

As the live auction began, I nudged David to raise our paddle for an Indian cooking class and dinner for twelve. He waited a few minutes, then held up our number, pushing the price to $800 and making us the winners. Energized, we bought the use of a new Mini Cooper for a weekend and four backstage passes to the Nutcracker. Then, it was time for the class projects to take the stand.

Works in progress for months, the class projects were the

crown jewels of the evening. Every teacher at the school had contributed an idea and every child had participated in the process of creation. There were wood-and-steel sculptures, tables with hand-painted tiles, mobiles of yarn and cloth, all meant to affirm the wonder of our offspring and certify how smart we were to be at the school. David and I had no need for a collection of papier-mâché animal masks displayed on a coat rack, but buying the creation Emily and her classmates had made was a good way to demonstrate our support, give to the science lab, and show how proud we were of our daughter, her teacher, and her classmates.

"We could keep the masks for a couple weeks, then distribute each one to its creator," I suggested. "Go slowly. Let's see what other people do."

As wine flowed and music blared, the auctioneer surfed the crowd, pointing from one table to the next. The price moved upwards $50 at a time until it reached $1,000, then slowly crept to $1,100, at which point, everyone in the room was looking at our table, the auctioneer pointing directly at us.

"Going once. Eleven hundred dollars. Going twice . . . Do I hear eleven hundred and fifty? For the school?"

Suddenly, the crowd's attention turned. Someone at the back of the room had entered the bidding. Looking around, I saw a man holding a paddle over his head, a determined expression on his face. The woman at his side had her hands over her eyes. Was he trying to prove himself? Was she nervous about spending too much? Was she embarrassed? Had they talked about this beforehand?

No longer interested in Emily's project, I reached for David's arm. We didn't need to prove how much we could give or grab more of the spotlight.

"Let them have it," I whispered.

I tugged at David's sleeve attempting to pull our paddle to the table.

"The school will get the money either way. That's what matters," I said.

But David kept our paddle high until the price reached $1,300 and we became the owners of sixteen animal masks and a coat rack.

Walking to the car in the dark, I looked down at the pavement.

"That was ugly," I said.

"Aren't you glad we got it?" David said. "Emily's going to be excited."

"I guess we can point to Emily," I said. "But what were *we* trying to prove?"

"We're going to give each family the mask their child made. Do you know the other couple that was bidding?"

"I've seen her at school, but I don't know her."

"Well, they'll end up getting their child's mask."

"Yeah. We're being so generous," I said. "More like playground bullies."

A few days later, thinking about the auction, I declared myself both generous and self-centered, proud we did our part, but aware we'd been shamelessly showing off too. Later still, in discovering the auction raised nearly half a million dollars, I wondered if the money was a testament to the generosity of our 300-student elementary school or if, by donating to the school where our children were attending, we were just a bunch of overly privileged families giving to ourselves.

When Ali started preschool and Emily entered first grade, a mother of a boy in Ali's new class asked to meet with David and me. With more experience, I would know what to expect. At the time, however, I was clueless. After we'd been chatting for a few minutes, this mother looked directly at me and asked us to consider making a $100,000 donation. I was shocked. One hundred thousand dollars was an incredibly large amount of money. I couldn't believe she was asking for so much.

Over the days that followed, I kept running into this other mom at pick-up and drop-off and found myself hoping to impress her. I wanted to contribute to the school and make a positive difference as a generous community member and likable parent. Again, with more experience, I would know that a donation intended to please or gain status didn't often bring the desired results. Giving was best done without expectations, especially of being liked. At the time, silently contemplating the gift, I dug deep into my motives and intentions. What was I hoping to achieve? Did I expect something in return? Did we get when we gave? Did altruism exist? Whether a good feeling, a way to avoid guilt, gain peace of mind, or check "good deed" off a list, giving had benefits. Charity could be self-serving.

As I continued to contemplate what I wanted to do and why, I began to worry about not having enough, and wondered how much impact we could make. There were so many wealthy families at UCDS. No matter how much we donated, other parents could give more. Should we give to a school with fewer resources? If we gave the amount requested to UCDS, what would we do the following year? Should we be donating a certain percentage of our yearly income and considering tax breaks? We needed a plan. We needed charitable goals. There was research to be done. I wanted to do giving right.

When David joined the board of the Seattle Girls' School, a new middle school for girls, my questioning and learning continued. Philanthropy had a language of its own. I hadn't known "development" meant raising funds, an "endowment" was a large pool of money, "capacity" referred to the depth of a person's ability to give, and donors needed to be "cultivated." It was surprising to hear how David's committee "targeted" potential donors by going through lists of names, commenting on each one, and coming up with a strategy for extracting the largest amount possible when making an "ask."

"We're friends with that family," a committee member might say. "He just had back surgery. We should wait until he's feeling better to approach them."

Moving down the list and pointing to another name, someone might suggest requesting a "major gift."

"They have huge capacity. Their third child just graduated from college. Tuition is no longer an issue. They're ready to start focusing on philanthropy. Who can reach out to them?"

"They live next door to my brother," someone might say. "I'll talk to my sister-in-law and find out what she knows."

In many ways, fundraising was calculated and businesslike. But it was highly emotional and personal too. After David's committee identified potential donors, they spent months building connections, holding evening talks about the school's mission to give underserved girls access to an excellent education, and meeting with people over lunch. They thought about "stewardship" as well, keeping their donors informed and helping them feel good about being involved in something bigger than themselves. After all, an informed, engaged donor was likely to give again.

While I was shocked by UCDS's ask, the $100,000 requested got me thinking bigger than I'd ever imagined, my idea of what was possible expanding exponentially. Thinking about the need for everyone in our country to have access to a good education, we decided to give UCDS twice as much as we'd ever given and earmark our $20,000 gift for financial aid. Months later, also in support of education, David suggested we make an even larger gift to provide scholarships to two underprivileged girls every year for the lifetime of the Seattle Girls' School.

"Let's donate $80,000 to the endowment," he said.

Twenty thousand dollars already felt like a generous amount. At first, it was hard to imagine letting go of four times as much. But, with my heart ready to give, and my head reminding me of enough, we added $80,000 to the endowment, which left me feeling proud, then humbled. It was gratifying to make a positive difference in other people's lives.

With increasing exposure to big numbers, larger gifts began to sound normal, and given the abundance in our life, I felt an increasing need and desire to give. Philanthropy became part of our social life too. Friends started to invite us to auctions and luncheons, asking for contributions to causes they cared about, proving peer pressure could be a positive force. In fact, in years to come, Bill and Melinda Gates, along with Warren

Buffett, would use peer pressure in creating The Giving Pledge to inspire other billionaires to donate their wealth to charity.

In 2002, David and I put $600,000 into a donor-advised fund. But it soon became clear that letting go of the cash was not the hardest part of philanthropy and far from the most rewarding. Although the money was no longer ours, I had no idea where to direct the funds. I wanted to reach outside our immediate community to support women and children. David wanted to do more to improve education. Neither of us had specific ideas or organizations in mind. Browsing the internet in search of worthy nonprofits was not the answer. There was no way to evaluate an organization based on a website. And without an emotional connection or knowing any of the people involved, I felt little impetus to give. In fact, for years, I was stuck. I felt guilty. I wanted to be doing more but wasn't sure where to start—and I let my obligations and responsibilities as a mother take precedence.

Years later, when the girls were older and I no longer felt the need for a grand plan or to do giving perfectly, I viewed philanthropy not only as an obligation and responsibility, but as a benefit and a joy. Giving was highly personal, an expression of my values, and a show of what I cared about most. Every gift was a statement about what was important to me. I felt fortunate to be able to donate $5,000, $10,000, and $20,000 to organizations that were doing good work and aligned with my values. When a gift had an impact and people were benefitting, I often gave again. Aware of our net worth and the abundance in my life, I didn't need to overthink philanthropy. I was doing giving my way. Meanwhile, my peers continued to help me increase my generosity. Many introduced me to organizations I wouldn't have discovered on my own, and I appreciated requests, often giving simply because I'd been asked. David was an inspiration too.

In 2010, David would cofound a nonprofit called Worldreader, giving people in the developing world access to digital books. He worked on the project full-time for three years without taking a salary, only paying himself once Worldreader began proving successful. Then, in 2015, David and I pledged a million-dollar gift to Worldreader, which was a milestone. Not long afterward, we made a second million-dollar pledge. And with Worldreader clearly helping to create a world where everyone had the books they needed to improve their lives, aware of the abundance in our own lives and hoping to inspire other potential donors to think bigger, we pledged five million dollars.

The people I spoke with about wealth were each at a different stage in their charitable thinking and giving, which meant a gift of $100 was as meaningful and generous to one person as a $100,000 gift was to another.

Loren, whose financial situation had changed dramatically after she met her boyfriend, spoke of how rewarding it was to give money to causes that were important to her.

"I visited an equestrian rescue farm with my mom last summer and ended up donating $250," she said. "My mom couldn't believe I could give so much. But it felt great, especially when the guy in charge told me it cost $250 a day to feed all the horses."

Laurie was worried she wasn't doing enough.

"We give to a couple places like the children's school, but I want to start doing more," she said. "I need to make the time. It's hard to know where to begin."

Meanwhile, after learning about charity from her children's schools, Julie had joined the board of a public school and was helping them raise money.

"The independent school my children attended taught me about philanthropy. I learned about things like capital campaigns," she said. "Over the years, I've made a commitment to myself never to give more in a year to our kids' schools than I give to the public schools."

Betsy had long been involved in charity, and when she and her husband wanted to start giving more, they determined how much to give their children, set a certain amount aside that allowed for their lifestyle, then put $30 million into a donor-advised fund with the intention of distributing the money over the coming fifteen years.

"I try to think locally, nationally, and internationally," Betsy said. "I'm most interested in women and education. I'm on a couple boards and have commitments to them. Over the years, we've given to our children's activities and interests too. Now, we give big to a couple of organizations and give smaller gifts of $5,000 and $10,000 to other places."

Denise, whose husband had sold his technology company when they were both in their mid-thirties, put $25 million into a family foundation the same year.

"We had so much," she said. "I needed a way to break the amount down and wanted to give it away myself. Too many foundations end up dispersing money once the founder has passed away. Where's the passion in other people blindly trying to figure out what I might have wanted or trying to adhere to restrictions once I'm gone? I wanted to make a difference in our community here and now."

For many years, Donna's financial advisor had budgeted an amount for her and Matt to give away every year.

"At the time, it was helpful to be told an amount," Donna said. "Having a set sum to give away got me to make a multi-year million-dollar pledge to women and girls through Women Moving Millions. But I don't think about charity that way anymore. Now, I get a sense of purpose through volunteering and making things happen in the nonprofit space and don't think about giving away a set sum."

Janet, who worked for her family foundation, set a goal for herself to give away ten percent of her salary, donating to organizations where she volunteered and giving smaller amounts to friends who asked for her support when running a marathon or raising money for a cause.

"Since my job is to help people with their philanthropy, it's important for me to experience what my donors are experiencing and to give away some of the money I'm earning," she said.

In the future, fundraising as a board member of a nonprofit arts organization, and both watching and helping David raise money for Worldreader, I would see how generous people could be but also how the amount a person gave wasn't necessarily correlated with their net worth. Most seemed to approach charity based on what they'd known growing up. And since giving was a skill that could be learned and improved, the amounts people gave often increased over time. Most gave locally to organizations run by people they knew or to causes that touched their hearts.

◆ ◆ ◆

Soon after we put $600,000 into a donor-advised fund, I came face-to-face with a scruffy-looking homeless man holding a bent cardboard sign and reaching his gloved hand toward our car. I stared straight ahead, relieved when the traffic light turned green and I could escape up the street.

"Why was that man standing there?" Emily asked from the back.

I was silent.

"Did he want money? Why didn't you give him any? Do you have money?" she asked.

"Yes, but I don't just give money to people on the street," I said.

"Why not? Is he hungry? Did his sign say he was hungry?"

"There are places he can get food," I said. "It's better to give to an organization that can help him. That way, all the dollars are put to good use—for food, a place to sleep, to find a job."

Halfheartedly congratulating myself on addressing Emily's questions, I continued toward home in our Volvo sedan, not feeling all that good about myself. That man probably wasn't going to find a job. Would he have anything to eat tonight? Why didn't I give him any money? I'd watched someone a couple of cars ahead hand him a few bills but hadn't considered giving him anything myself. Like the caregiver at Emily's old daycare who empathized with the baristas, other drivers probably empathized more readily with the hardship he was facing. I'd read that people like me, who didn't have much direct contact with adversity or need, tended to lack compassion. I didn't want to be *that* person, following my own larger philanthropic agenda without opening my heart to those around me.

A few days later, when we were having dinner with Donna and Matt, I told them about the homeless man.

"I've never given money to people on the street," I said. "I was raised to believe it wasn't good to give to beggars. But that's not very compassionate. Next time I pass someone, I'm going to give them some money."

"We should all be more generous," Donna said. "Why don't we challenge ourselves? We could give gifts to unsuspecting strangers."

"Random acts of kindness," David said.

"What do you mean?" Matt asked. "We can't just walk up and down the street handing out cash."

"Let's each give away a thousand dollars," Donna said. "One hundred dollars at a time."

"I want to look another person in the eye and give from my heart," I said. "But it makes me nervous. Giving money feels so intimate, so vulnerable. Will people be suspicious? What if they refuse to take the money?"

"I don't think it'll be an issue. People will be happy," Donna said. "I'd like a hundred bucks for free."

A few weeks later, on a cold, drizzling evening, David and I stopped at a Christmas tree lot with Emily and Ali. A grey-haired man wearing a red-and-black flannel shirt and a clear plastic rain poncho, pointed out several trees, fluffing out the branches. We made our selection quickly, and the girls and I returned to the car while the tree guy sawed the end off of our tree and hoisted it onto the roof with David's help.

"That guy looks cold," Emily said.

"It's wet outside," Ali said.

When David opened the driver's door and leaned in to get his wallet, the two of us looked at one another and nodded.

A few minutes later, David jumped into the car.

"I did it!"

"What happened?" I asked.

"I paid for the tree then handed the guy a hundred-dollar bill. At first, he just looked at the money. When he understood it was for him, he was so happy. It made his day. Mine too."

The following week, with a hundred-dollar bill folded in the pocket of my dark purple coat, I walked into the dry cleaners to the sound of the bell and smell of hot wool. After paying and picking up the clothes, hardly noticing the metal hangers digging into my palm and not worrying about the dangers of plastic bags, I focused all my energy on getting the timing right.

"Happy Holidays!" I practically shouted, handing the woman a hundred dollars.

After years of greetings and pleasantries, it was as though the two of us saw each other for the first time. We stared. I smiled. She nodded.

"Thank you very much," she said.

"You're welcome," I said. "Thank *you*. It's always a pleasure to come in here."

Then I scurried out the door.

That evening, when I told David about the experience, his face contorted.

"I gave some money away today too," he said. "You know the woman at Starbucks?"

"The one who makes perfect latte foam?" I asked. "You gave her a hundred dollars?"

"I did," he said. "But, well, I went in there, planning to tell her what a great barista she was, but there was a long line. So, I waited around."

"Did she notice you?"

"I'm sure she did. I was hanging out, looking at espresso machines for quite a long time. Finally, I got a coffee as an excuse to talk to her," he said. "But it was like a comedy. Just as I got up to the counter, she went over to arrange things on the shelves."

"What did you do?"

"It was so awkward."

"Why didn't you just leave?"

"I should have. But I was determined. I went over and let her know that we thought she was a great barista and handed her a hundred dollars. But she refused to take it."

"Oh no!"

"Yeah, it was bad," he said, beginning to laugh. "It got worse. I didn't give up. I insisted. Finally, she told me to put the money in the tip jar."

"Did you?"

"Yes . . . and ran out of the store."

Several weeks later, David had more success. On our way to Napa, we stopped at an In-N-Out Burger. David placed our order while Emily, Ali, and I found a table and arranged napkins, ready for our meal. Suddenly, David was standing by my side, asking for one of our special bills. I handed him a hundred dollars and watched him hurry back to the counter where he stopped in front of a young couple. He said something to the woman then handed her the bill. She covered her mouth and began hopping up and down, while the man pumped David's hand, a huge smile on his face.

"When I was paying for the food, I needed ten cents," David told me when he returned to the table. "I was fishing around in my pocket, trying to come up with the change and that guy gave me a dime."

"And you gave him a hundred dollars?"

"That's right. Did you see his reaction?"

"He looked ecstatic," I said. "He looked the way this makes me feel."

I had no idea what a hundred dollars meant to the couple or what they would do with the money, but I felt connected to them, our lives touching for a warm, happy moment. The element of surprise was joyous too. Whether a dime, a dollar, or a hundred, being charitable was not about amounts or philanthropic strategy but about opening our hearts and doing our personal best to make a positive difference in one another's lives.

Contemplation & Conversation

- What did you learn about giving during your childhood? Has your attitude toward giving changed? If so, how and why?

- Do you give enough? What does enough mean in this context? Do you think of yourself as generous? Does peer pressure affect your giving?

- What do you gain when you give? What keeps you giving or stops you from giving again?

Chapter Fourteen

EMOTIONS ATTACHED

G oing out for dinner with friends, David and I didn't always pick up the tab. Sometimes we paid, other times we didn't, and often the cost got split down the middle. The bill wasn't a problem with friends who shared our circumstances. Even with those who didn't, the cost of dinner was rarely an issue. When it came to travelling with other families, however, we had to think ahead and plan carefully to avoid awkward moments. Mostly, we did what we could to stay within other people's budgets. But when we wanted to go big or do something exotic, it was surprisingly difficult to give—and receive—financial gifts.

As we considered a trip to the Galapagos, we asked Tracy and Ethan, parents from UCDS, if they wanted to join us. Emily and Ali got along well with their kids and we liked the idea of having an adventure as two families. Tracy and Ethan liked the idea too. Soon, all of us were looking forward to spending time together, excited to learn about Darwin, and eager to see blue-footed boobies. But as Tracy and I talked about specifics and decided on a travel company, I realized that the trip was expensive.

"I hope we haven't pushed Tracy and her family into an uncomfortably high-priced vacation," I said to David.

Offering to pay for everything felt presumptuous and wasn't what either David or I wanted. We didn't know Tracy and Ethan well. Even offering to pay a portion of the cost felt awkward. Relationships were best when they were equal and balanced. I didn't want to come across as patronizing or as making a statement about their financial situation. I didn't want to ignore our situation either. I wanted to share with our friends. But would they be embarrassed if we offered to help? Maybe they'd feel resentful if we didn't offer. It was hard to know. Any move we made, or didn't make, had implications that would be difficult to clarify.

Hoping to help defray the cost of the vacation without being over-the-top, we decided to offer to buy the airline tickets for the flights from the mainland to the island. Getting the tickets seemed like an easy, concrete way to for us to acknowledge our good fortune and do something nice for our friends. So, with a plan in place, I picked up the phone. But before I could even finish explaining our wish to cover the cost of the tickets, Tracy cut me off, declining graciously but definitively. Unsure how to explain our intentions without sounding argumentative or defensive, I let the issue drop. Later, when Tracy discovered there were only two cabins available on the boat's middle deck and called to ask if her family could take them, I saw another opportunity. Since we had already reserved upper deck cabins, I suggested we upgrade her family.

"That way, we could all be together on the same deck," I said.

"That's nice of you," she said. "But we'll take the middle deck.

I'm just glad you got us to go on this trip. We're looking forward to it."

Had they already considered the top deck and decided against it? Maybe they felt it was odd to let us pay extra for them. Perhaps they preferred to keep finances outside of our relationship and time together. It could have been pride. It could have been embarrassment. It could have been something between Tracy and her husband or something about David and me. Perhaps it was nothing. Without asking directly, there was no way to know.

I wasn't sure how often our financial circumstances skewed social interactions but I was upset when a friend told me she'd been afraid to ask our family to join hers at a Cirque du Soleil show. I'd been so happy she'd invited us.

"I knew you could sit in the best seats," she said. "Since we couldn't afford front row, I almost didn't ask you. I thought about it a lot. I was worried you wouldn't want to go if you had to sit in bad seats."

I felt badly for having been unaware of my friend's concern. My feelings were hurt too. Our friendship meant more to me than front row seats. Didn't she know that? Didn't she feel the same? I hadn't realized our wealth played such an outsized role in her mind.

"It's awkward to travel with rich friends," my friend Leslie told me. "Last year, a couple we knew was excited about a trip they were taking to Morocco. They were staying in penthouse suites in the best hotels, taking exclusive tours, meeting influential people. They had all kinds of special drivers lined up to take them around. So, when they asked us to go with them, I panicked. We couldn't afford to travel like that. I was debating what to say when my friend told me we could go as their guests, that everything was lined up. So, we stayed in the hotel down the street, but got to experience first-class travel."

"Sounds great."

"Well, yes and no," Leslie said. "Now I have a problem. Those same friends want us to vacation with them in Tahiti. It would be presumptuous to expect them to pay a second time, but I'm too embarrassed to say we can't afford the trip. I've been avoiding the subject, being noncommittal. I don't think they're aware that the cost is an issue for us," Leslie said. "I've been stalling so long I've hurt their feelings. They think we don't want to go with them."

"Why don't you explain?"

"I want to be an equal," Leslie said. "I guess I'd rather have them think we don't want to go with them than let them know we can't afford to keep up."

Later, Laurie told me she was upset by how her new wealth had impacted one of her oldest friendships.

"My best friend and I biked together for years, but she's stopped racing with me. She said it was too expensive, that it was easy for me because I didn't have to think about the cost," Laurie said. "But most people who race don't have a lot of money. It feels like she's using our money as an excuse not to spend time with me."

Sue said her friendships had become self-sorting. Over the

years, she had grown closest to people who shared her circumstances.

"It's nice to go out for dinner without having to worry about the cost, to know price isn't an issue for anyone at the table," she said.

Allison didn't think her closest friendships had changed, but she noticed subtle comments.

"People say things about me driving a Range Rover or about how 'tough' it must be that I quit my job," she said. "They say these things in a joking manner, but it can be hurtful."

She was also surprised by the response on social media to her husband's success.

"When he was starting his business, when he was the underdog, so many people were rooting for him. Once he'd sold the business and was doing well, friends stopped cheering him on. The number of people liking his posts went way down. I don't think the drop in support was out of malice, but we noticed it."

Loren had a similar experience with her closest friend.

"When I suddenly had money, the dynamic between us changed," she said. "She'd always been the one with the nice clothes. Then, when I got a Louis Vuitton bag and started shopping at Barneys, she reminded me she'd had nice things first. It hurt my feelings. I wanted her to be excited for me. I think she was worried she'd lost control of me or that I didn't need her in the same way. It took a year for us to work it out."

When Julie's husband proposed, she'd been stunned. Like me, she hadn't been contemplating diamonds. Unlike me, she felt guilty her ring was so large.

"At first, I was just shocked," she said. "Then I was embarrassed."

Right after getting engaged, she and her husband visited her husband's parents, where her husband's brother, who had also just gotten engaged, joined them for dinner with his fiancée.

"Her ring didn't look anything like mine," Julie said. "I kept turning my ring around on my finger, trying to hide it, but I knew the subject would come up."

Eventually, her husband's family asked to see her ring. "Wow!" they said. "It's so big!"

"I felt bad. My sister-in-law didn't say anything or seem upset, but I felt awful," Julie said. "It's taken years for me to stop feeling apologetic. Sometimes I still take my ring off and don't wear it around certain friends or to certain events."

Carla, my friend from PEPS, and I rediscovered tennis together. Neither of us had been on the court in years, but after hitting the ball around one morning, we were both excited to be back in the game. Soon, we were playing as often as possible, scheduling time at public indoor courts not far from where we lived—and I found myself dreaming of the Seattle Tennis Club.

Nestled along the shore of Lake Washington, the Seattle Tennis Club was known as *the* place to serve and volley. Since it was known for serving up plenty of snob appeal as well, I'd never considered joining. But hoping to meet other players, I looked into membership. When I did, the $10,000 initiation fee was not a surprise. Neither was the ten-year waiting list or the fact that a current member needed to sponsor my application. But I was appalled to learn our family had to be endorsed by ten members and that everyone at the club would ultimately vote on whether we could join. It was just as I'd always feared and imagined. Private clubs were for aloof people who wanted to keep away from the riffraff.

I called Donna. "It's so pretentious," I complained.

"You wouldn't believe what a woman from our daughter's school told me," Donna said. "She's a member, and when I asked about joining, she told me I'd need a sponsor."

"Couldn't she have been your sponsor?"

"Exactly," Donna said. "I asked her. She said she didn't know enough about our family and refused to recommend us!"

Hearing this, even though Ms. Old Money offered to sponsor our family and David and I knew many members who could endorse our application, I didn't add our name to the list. With David speculating we could buy our way in without waiting ten years, I ran even faster in the opposite direction, somewhat relieved to reject the Seattle Tennis Club before it could reject me. The club may have been a sanctuary for its members with its perfectly maintained indoor and outdoor courts, kid-friendly sandy beach, and outdoor swimming pool, but I wanted to play tennis and to play with Carla.

Many years later, when we moved to San Francisco and I was again interested in playing tennis, I had no problem joining a private club. There was a great place just blocks from our house. While the price made the club exclusive, there was no waiting list or all-member vote. Mostly, more comfortable with wealth, I was grateful to have a nice facility so close to where we lived.

At the time, back in Seattle, Carla and I continued to hit. We signed up for lessons, joined a United States Tennis Association team, and began to talk about getaways—which had me dreaming again. I loved the idea of going somewhere sunny and warm for a week and spending time learning from a pro. But my ability to afford a high-end tennis camp didn't do me much good. I didn't want to go alone. I wanted to go with Carla—and was thrilled when she told me she'd discovered a reasonably priced clinic in Palm Springs that coincided with a major tournament in Indian Wells and suggested we go together.

The hotel near the clinic was the obvious place to stay, but Carla didn't want to spend too much, and again, I was concerned that money would come between us—until I finally embraced the facts. I booked a large room at the nearby hotel, and told Carla she could be my guest. When I did, no chasm opened. There wasn't even a crack. In fact, in acknowledging my ability to pay, I felt closer to Carla. She was thankful, too.

Several years later, as Carla and I talked about attending a tennis tournament in Barcelona, I told her I wanted to pay her airfare.

"It's easy for me to do," I wrote in an email.

"I've been trying to figure out why your offer makes me uncomfortable," Carla wrote back. "I'm afraid that if you buy me the ticket, it will make our relationship out of balance and you'll think less of me. I don't want to be weak or a sponger—or feel like a child. Adults take care of children, and then resent it . . . and as soon as I step back from that statement, I see how fear-driven it is and how much it's rooted in the past and not in current truths. As you said, it's easy for you, and we can spend time together. It should be that simple."

Luckily, for both of us, Carla set her worries aside and

accepted the ticket, allowing us to spend seven wonderful days together watching Rafa Nadal win all his matches.

◆ ◆ ◆

Navigating friendships and financial gifts was tricky. Having friends ask us directly for money was even harder.

One evening, after going out for drinks with a friend, David burst through the front door, apologizing for being late.

"I was having quite a conversation with Bob," he said.

"What about?"

"I don't know what to do," he said.

David shook his head, prolonging the suspense, holding onto the secret and waiting for me to guess. But I had no idea. Finally, he told me Bob had asked him for a loan of $25,000.

Imagining Bob in his striped button-down shirts, creased khakis, and leather loafers, I was baffled. His family took overseas vacations and went skiing every year. They'd just purchased a new car and their kids attended private school. Our families had spent time and money together over fancy dinners and luxurious weekends. Bob's need for a loan didn't add up.

"They're in debt," he continued. "They're spending more than they're bringing in. The bank won't lend them anything. Their personal finances and business expenses are all mixed up. It's been going on for years."

"Will $25,000 make a difference?" I asked. "Won't it add to their problem?"

"They don't see their situation as a problem. I feel bad about saying, 'No.' But I don't feel good about loaning them money."

David had recently given $10,000 to an acquaintance who was going through a rough time, and that gift had been complicated to give.

"There are no strings attached," David had said. "I expect nothing in return."

"It's too generous," his acquaintance had told him. "But I'll give it some thought."

A couple of days later, his acquaintance called David to say he'd been discussing the situation with his brother and couldn't possibly accept the money. The day after that, he got another call.

"I'll take you up on your offer," his acquaintance said. "Thank you."

But giving money to someone on the periphery of our life was far less fraught with emotion and complexity than giving a loan to a close friend. The situation with Bob was complicated by years of family dinners and weekend trips we hoped would continue.

"I'll offer to help Bob come up with a plan for his business," David said. "Then, when things are on track, I'll give him the money he needs."

Several months later, when I asked how Bob was doing, David said the subject of money had disappeared.

"He's not willing or able to look at his business. I don't think he wants to make any changes."

"Can you help him figure it out?"

"I could, but it's his business, not mine."

"But he made it your business when he asked for $25,000," I said. "Do you think Bob was using your friendship?"

"No. He didn't want to ask. And I don't mind that he did,"
David said.

David's friendship with Bob endured without any perceivable repercussions. There was no change in the relationship our families shared either. But without discussing the subject, it was hard to know for sure what feelings existed beneath the surface. I couldn't deny being more aware of the money Bob and his wife spent. And when Bob asked us for money again several years later, we gave him the cash outright, telling him to view the money as a gift he could keep.

Not long after Bob asked for money the first time, another family whose children were in school with Emily and Ali sent an email to a small group of relatively affluent families, telling us they were hundreds of thousands of dollars in debt, needed help, and would likely never be able to repay the money. This information was a complete surprise. With three children in private school, a big home, and hired help, the couple appeared to be doing well. For a few days, everyone on the email tried to make sense of the situation, sharing confusion and concern, unsure what to do. Then, silence prevailed. Although the request was strange and impersonal, David and I decided to send a $10,000 check. How could we not do something? I'd spent time on the tennis court with the woman and David had gotten to know her husband through evening gatherings. Their children were in school with ours. We were in a position to help.

Weeks after we'd sent the gift, when I received a two-sentence thank you note—no call, no gushing, no further reaching out, I became painfully aware of the strings I'd attached to our gift.

I wanted more appreciation. Unconsciously hoping for more closeness, I was hurt to be treated like a bank, rather than a person, let alone a friend.

Later, Janet shared her way of dealing with the emotional stress of being asked for money.

"My therapist, of all people, asked me for a loan," she told me. "She promised to pay me back, but never did. Now, I think about the money I gave her as the fund I loan people. Although no one else has asked for that money, if anyone does, I'll tell them to find my ex-therapist. She still has the money I'm willing to give away as a loan."

◆   ◆   ◆

When my brother was buying a house, and David and I offered to add $20,000 to his down payment, he refused our gift—which I tried not to take personally.

"I want to live within my own means," he told me.

Although he didn't accept money as a single man, when we wrote my brother a $20,000 check as a wedding present, he and his wife accepted with thanks. And when he and his wife had their first child and we sent $20,000, he again thanked us. We then started to send money every year. But after a while, my brother stopped acknowledging our gifts, and my feelings were hurt once again. Although I knew I should speak up, it made me uncomfortable to broach the topic. I didn't want to make a big deal of his silence or create conflict. We were living in different countries and didn't talk often. It was also easy for me to imagine how he felt. Maybe he was self-conscious about accepting money he hadn't earned, or perhaps he considered money easy for me to give and therefore not worth mentioning. But over time, hearing nothing but silence, I began to feel taken for granted. Although not completely conscious of the decision or proud of the fact, one year, I didn't send $20,000.

That next January, as my brother and I were conversing over email, he ended his note with, "Hoping a certain year-end gift is just slow in the mail—is it?" Seeing these words, I froze, shocked and angry then embarrassed and ashamed. I should have spoken up years earlier, given him a chance to explain, and let him know how I felt. Even though the idea of talking to him about money made me nervous, I knew it had to happen.

Getting clear about my feelings and thinking through how to express them, I realized how much my brother meant to me. I wanted him to know I cared about him and his family. It didn't matter what he did with the cash, but hearing only silence, I felt as though our money was simply disappearing, unappreciated, into a void. My brother's silence also made our choice to send money feel like an obligation. Did he view money as being nothing to us? Did he believe our gifts were foregone conclusions? I wanted him to know there were emotions attached, that I was making a decision to send money, and that he was important to me.

Once we were on the phone, when I told him I was upset he hadn't thanked me, he apologized immediately. He hadn't known my feelings were hurt and explained he had consciously tried to keep things low-key, that he purposely hadn't said much about the money because he thought I didn't want him to make a big deal of it.

"I thought it was more comfortable for you if I didn't say anything," he told me.

I'd had no idea. Had I given him that impression? His thinking seemed to be a relic from our childhood, making me realize again that I loved him. He then told me he didn't need the money, but that it had always been very much appreciated. The next day, I sent him $20,000.

Navigating the imbalance of wealth with immediate and extended family was a source of confusion, upset, and joy for all the people I interviewed.

Sue had purchased two separate houses for her divorced parents and was charging them each a small amount in rent so things wouldn't, in her words, "get weird."

"It happened organically," she said. "When the place across the street from us went on the market, it made sense for my mom. After that, we decided to get a place for my dad too. I think they are both more comfortable paying a little every month."

Laurie's husband had started his business with his brother, but over time, his brother's personal problems had begun to affect his work.

"He wasn't doing well in the business," Laurie said. "My husband tried boosting him up, giving him opportunities to succeed, but he was on a downward spiral. We sent him to top rehab facilities for his addictions, but it didn't work. It's been hard on my husband and his parents. I feel awful for my sister-in-law. The situation probably would have been the same even if we didn't have so much money, but our wealth makes things even more intense. There's so much blame, resentment, and guilt."

She felt judged by her siblings too.

"Maybe it's my issue, but I get stressed about birthday gifts," she said. "My sisters seem to expect something big. I never know what to do. Their expectations make me feel as though a nice new shirt isn't good enough."

"My husband has six siblings," Denise said. "For several years, we gave each one of them a financial gift. But my husband and I decided to stop sending them money. One of his brothers squandered everything we gave him. The others didn't need our help."

"We set up an education fund for our twelve nieces and nephews," Betsy said. "I think it's easier to give and receive money when it's attached to a value. We're giving education. Everyone has welcomed the gift."

Betsy also talked about organizing a family vacation where she flew thirty members of her extended family to Montana and paid for the resort. While everyone seemed happy to be part of the festivities, she was uncomfortable with her mother's reaction.

"She was too deferential, too polite and overly thankful. It made me uneasy," Betsy said. "Money is power. But I ended up getting angry at her. We'd made sacrifices to accommodate the dates, and then my mom ended up leaving a day early. She just took off."

In general, Betsy was happy to use her resources to help family members, but she could get frustrated too.

"My sister complains about not having enough money," Betsy said. "Then, she tells me about all the trips she's taking with friends. All I can do is listen, but I'm thinking, 'Can you afford that?' or '*Another* special weekend?'"

Betsy was even more upset by her aunt's situation.

"My aunt makes one bad decision after another," Betsy said. "She has three big dogs but can barely feed herself. She's now on the verge of homelessness. I wonder where my responsibility lies in all of it. Her three daughters aren't doing anything. Since I have resources, is it my duty to help? I've given and lent her money many, many times, but now my mom is telling me I shouldn't give her anything more."

Karen's brother, who had problems with drugs, often asked her for money.

"He'd call when his electricity was about to get turned off," Karen said. "I'd tell him I'd give him money under certain conditions, and he complained about having strings attached. But there had to be some quid pro quo. He was an adult. I didn't want him buying drugs or alcohol with money from me."

Karen also gave money to her brother's ex-wife.

"I'd been thinking of it as money to help with basic expenses," she said. "It was hard to hear her tell me she was taking a vacation to Africa. I wasn't going on a vacation in Africa. Was that what she was doing with the money I'd given her?"

Another woman with four siblings, each with families of their own, told me she was upset by the family dynamics around vacations. Three of her siblings were happy to accept invitations from her and her husband to gather on Cape Cod, but one of her brothers and his wife refused to join them.

"I think it's my sister-in-law," she said. "She told me she didn't feel comfortable in *that* setting, like it was too high-end and therefore unpleasant. My brother hasn't been very nice about it either. He just says he's not coming. Maybe he's resentful.

I'm not sure what to do. It means our whole family never gets together."

"One of my sisters struggles with our lifestyle," Nicole said. "She makes snarky comments, wondering why exactly I'm working or saying things like, 'You're redoing your kitchen, *again*?' I've learned not to talk about our travel or remodels with her. We talk about world issues instead."

Janet and her siblings had all inherited wealth, but each had different priorities.

"My sister buys a lot of clothes and purses, which I can't imagine being able to afford," Janet said. "But after comparing my sister's spending to my own, I realize I blow a lot of money on airplane tickets and hotels. I never go business class, but I do travel a lot."

David and I gave $10,000 to one of his aunts who was going through a hard time, $50,000 to his godfather as a no-interest loan, $20,000 to his brother for a down payment on a house, and $20,000 to his mother for a special vacation, putting two pieces of red yarn in the envelope with the check to prove there were no strings attached. But we didn't have a long-term plan for giving to our parents—until David's mother told him she was anxious about her finances.

"She's worried about running out of money," he said. "I've looked at her accounts. She's doing fine. But I want to do something. I don't want her to worry."

We'd taken his mother on trips, sent airline tickets, and thrown her a party for a big birthday, but David felt uncomfortable giving her cash.

"It's strange," he said. "It's a weird, unnatural role reversal. I'm not sure how much would keep her from worrying. One hundred thousand dollars?"

"Not more?"

A friend had once told me she preferred the "one-time drop," that she didn't like the idea of yearly gifts or transactions because they could start to feel like entitlements or obligations. It sounded easiest to give David's mom one large sum. But it was hard to know the right amount. There were no guidelines around how much to give your parents and we couldn't peek over the fence at our friends and use their gifts as benchmarks. We knew Donna and Matt and Lynn and Adam took their parents and extended family on vacations, but we didn't know more. Although the six of us had been friends for years and were in similarly fortunate financial situations, there was an unspoken understanding between us that talk of money was off limits. Discussing specifics just wasn't done.

"We could give my mom a million dollars," David said. "But it would make her happier if I called her every day."

In the end, we decided to give her $20,000. We then began sending that same amount every year and continued doing so for over a decade. But when she wanted to make a move, and we bought her a condominium in Florida, we stopped the yearly gifts—and we all felt better about a "one-time drop."

Thinking about giving money to my parents, I was still stuck in the past. For years, we'd all abided by old rules, never speaking of finances. My parents never questioned our spending or acknowledged our growing wealth. After years of watching my father whisk bills from restaurant tables as my mother looked away and Michael and I were supposed to do the same, bringing up the subject of money felt like I'd be pushing my dad's hand aside, grabbing for the check, and paying with hundred-dollar bills. Disrupting the status quo felt rebellious and disrespectful. A conversation about money would also confirm my role in our family had changed. But with a plan in place for giving to David's mom, I wanted to do the same for my parents. So, I summoned my courage and asked my father out for coffee.

After ordering lattes, sitting down at a table, and chatting about the weather, I told my dad that we wanted to start giving him and my mom $20,000 a year.

"It will be something you can count on and use any way you want," I said.

There was silence. But he didn't frown. He didn't stand up in a huff, spill his drink, or keel over in shock. He smiled.

"That's very nice, honey. Thank you," he said. "This is good coffee."

We sat in silence, watching people at the counter.

"For our next vacation, maybe your mother and I will go business class," he said.

Since my father had always been the financial manager in our family, I never considered talking to my mother first. But after successfully sharing a coffee and telling my dad about the money we wanted to give him, I had my first conversation about finances with my mom.

"Thank you, darling," she said. "Your father is so pleased."

"You're welcome. I know Dad worries."

"We never expected you to give us anything. You and David are being very generous."

"I was nervous about giving you money," I admitted.

"Well, it's a wonderful gift," she reassured me. "Your father is already having fun spending it in his head."

"I'm glad. I wasn't sure how you felt about me having so much."

"You're doing so well with it," my mother said. "I'm proud."

Despite myself, in her approval, I heard judgment.

"You are spending so wisely. You don't live in a McMansion. I remember Mother's wealthy friends. My parents never liked the way they spent their money. They lived in big, showy homes, led flashy lives, drank too much . . ."

"They had such an influence. You were so nervous around those friends."

My mother was silent.

"In my mother's generation, real ladies weren't supposed to talk about, or even think about, money," she said. "When I was growing up, women didn't work unless they had to. Mother was lucky. She didn't need a job. She could leave finances up to my father. I guess I'm a bit old-fashioned. I leave the finances up to your father. If I need anything, I ask him. He wouldn't have it any other way. Neither would I."

"Growing up, I thought money was dirty, that I wasn't supposed to talk about it."

"You've always been so interested in money," she said.

Trying not to hear criticism again, I stayed quiet.

"It's taken years for me to feel at ease with our wealth," I finally said. "You and Dad taught me good habits around managing finances and not spending too much. Even now, I identify with being frugal and managing my money well. But it's taken years to feel okay about being rich."

"Well, you are doing a good job," she said again. "And it's nice of you to share. We certainly didn't expect it."

"We're happy to do it," I said. And I meant it.

"It's in your father's genes to worry," she continued. "Your father and I make a good pair. Even if we had more money, your father would worry, and I'd have trouble buying things."

"I completely understand," I said. And I meant that too.

Contemplation & Conversation

- Does money play a role in your friendships?

- What experiences have you had giving money to or receiving money from family members?

- Have you run into money issues with your siblings? How do your siblings feel about your financial standing?

- How has money impacted your relationship with your parents? Have you talked with them about money? Have you ever given them money?

- Do you judge people based on their financial decisions? Do you feel judged by others?

Chapter Fifteen

IMPERFECTION

I n February 2002, David worked his last day at Amazon. That evening, believing the two of us were going out for a quiet dinner with Donna and Matt, he was greeted by "Surprise!" as we walked into the restaurant. I'd organized a party. Colleagues, friends, and family had gathered in his honor. His uncle, the minister who married us, had flown to Seattle from North Carolina. His old roommate from Boston, the guy who drank his orange juice and left the empties in the fridge, was present too. So was his buddy with whom he'd biked across the country. Childhood friends and classmates from high school, college, and business school; employees and managers from Microsoft and Amazon; his mother, brother, half brothers, stepmother, and my parents—all were there to acknowledge and celebrate his hard work and success.

"I'd work for you anytime," a woman from Amazon announced in a toast.

"You are my role model and hero," someone else proclaimed.

More than a hundred voices filled the room with good cheer. People shared stories and funny anecdotes, singing David's praise. But a silent question hovered like a blimp. No one asked it aloud. No one dared say the word. It was inappropriate and impolite to suggest retirement. The very idea of not working at the age of thirty-six was vaguely distasteful, running counter to social norms. David himself had no intention of retiring. And with the idea triggering questions about money and wealth, silence prevailed, at least around David and me.

When people asked David what he was going to do with his time, sometimes he talked about our five-year plan, saying he wanted to teach and give himself space to find his next Big Thing. Other times, he explained he planned to divide his life into thirds: one for family, one for self-improvement, and one for volunteering. Either way, I was proud of his accomplishments and success, as well as of his courage to leave the known path to do something new. The next chapter of our lives was beginning. Not many people knew, but something else was hovering like a blimp—me. I was pregnant again.

At first, when the alarm on David's side of the bed didn't go off on Monday morning, I wondered what he would do with his day. Would he mess up my schedule and interfere in my routine? But during the first week he was at home, I was the one nosing into his business.

"What are you doing?" I asked, walking into our bedroom where he was rummaging through his dresser.

"Looking for running shorts," he said.

A runner myself, I'd never had success getting him to join me for a jog. He'd always dismissed the idea and jumped on his bike. Yet, there he was, holding up a pair of bright blue shorts that reminded me of the day we met at Microsoft eleven years earlier.

"Want to join me?" he asked.

Jogging along the sidewalk next to David, I had a hard time keeping my pace slow enough to stay by his side. But he didn't care. Challenging himself in a whole new way, he was planning to run a marathon in the fall. He also put on the old houndstooth sports jacket he'd worn to propose, walked down the street to the University of Washington, and taught a class at the business school called Competing on the Internet. Meanwhile, I crawled into bed, exhausted from the pregnancy and very happy to have David at home. He was a big help with the girls in the morning and became part of their afternoon routine.

When I was five months along, I woke with a jolt. There was blood on the sheets. No longer unaware that pregnancy could end badly, I called my doctor in a panic. An hour later, sitting next to David in the waiting room with my hands on my stomach, I avoided looking at pregnant women and didn't watch the fish. When we were called into my doctor's office, she asked me to lie down. Then, after getting out the heart rate monitor, she probed my stomach, searching for our baby's heartbeat while David squeezed my hand. I stared at the light. It was taking way too long.

"Is he okay?" I asked. "Is everything alright?"

We already knew the baby was a boy. We had named him Max, excited to be having a son and for Emily and Ali to have a little brother. Finally, as the monitor found its target, the room filled with the whirring of Max's heart.

"Things sound fine," my doctor said. "But let's do an ultrasound."

After taking a thorough look, she confirmed all was well. Then, assuring us that spotting could be normal, she sent us home. A week later, during a dinner of chicken with caramelized onions, apricots, and prunes, the bleeding started again. This time, it didn't stop.

David got the girls into bed while I cried in the bathroom. Once in bed myself, I kept my hands on my stomach as Max fluttered within me. I told him how much I loved him and that I wouldn't let him go. But early in the morning, while the room was still dark, contractions began, and when my water broke, David called an ambulance that took me to the hospital. Max didn't survive.

Alone in a hospital room for two days, consumed with a grief too powerful for phone calls and too intense for visitors, I barely registered David's visits. Sometimes he brought Emily and Ali and they bounced on the bed, but they didn't stay long.

David brought me home to a kitchen full of flowers. No baby. Just flowers. Our glass-top table was covered with white lilies and bright daisies, pink wildflowers and lavender blossoms. In my sadness, I took pictures and imagined showing them to Max, pointing out the pretty colors. I would show him when he was old enough. When he could understand. Maybe when he was five or six. That way, he could see how many people cared and how much he was loved. Every day, more sympathy notes and warm wishes arrived, and I added them to the kitchen table and took more photos, thinking about Max.

When the vases were gone and the glass-top table was empty, I understood Max would never see the flowers. He would never see the pictures. He would never know how much he was missed or feel how much he was loved. He would never be five.

He would never be in my arms—and the thought opened me to so much sorrow that I thought I might shatter.

◆　◆　◆

The summer after losing Max, we retreated to Napa Valley. Pulling into the driveway of our remodeled house was like driving right into the cover of *Country Home*. Newly planted shrubs framed the beautiful yellow Victorian. A gray flagstone path edged in white tea roses led to the wraparound front porch and dark green door. A butler could have appeared from within, holding a tray of milk and cookies and a story for the girls. Everything looked perfect.

I walked up the front stairs, through the door and into the living room, touching the cream-colored cashmere throw draped on the back of an armchair and noting the white orchids on the coffee table. The scent of an amber candle drifted through the room. Cheryl and Marla, our designers, had worked magic. Every piece of furniture was perfectly arranged. I stared toward the back at the lawn and sparkling pool while Emily and Ali ran upstairs, excited to play on their bunk beds. Turning to David, I pulled him close. The house was gorgeous, but I couldn't escape the hole I felt within.

That summer, the minute my eyes opened every morning, I thought of Max. Looking over, I knew David was thinking about him too. There was nothing we could do. All the begging and bartering couldn't change reality. I couldn't will a different outcome.

When it came to the house, even after trying to do rich right, after throwing my weight and money around, I hadn't actually achieved perfection. In fact, the closer perfect seemed to be getting, the further away it felt. Although the pool house fit nicely within the backyard and the pool was an ideal depth for young children, mistakes had been made—and the defects were glaring. There were cracks in the poured concrete near the grill. The wood beams in the kitchen ceiling were uneven. The paint color in the dining room was too dark. I was frustrated by the fancy oven that supposedly doubled as a microwave but took five minutes to boil a cup of water.

"I don't know why the architect didn't put our master bedroom at the back of the house so we'd have a view," David complained.

Hearing this, I nodded. I agreed. But I laughed. It was easier to see David's folly than my own. With him picking at a detail, failing to appreciate the beauty of our home, I knew our perspective had to change. It was easy to believe that wealth had the power to fix every problem and that a massive remodel could create perfection, but neither was true. The house was beautiful, but life couldn't be controlled. Happiness wasn't engineered. Joy did not come with a bedroom in the right place. Money didn't change everything. All those expectations were only making me feel worse.

When Emily, Ali, and I made lemonade, squeezing lemons and measuring sugar, rather than having fun with the process and enjoying time with the girls, I focused on the limestone counters.

"Use a sponge," I barked at Emily. "Wipe up all the juice. The acid will leave white marks."

Sitting by the pool, watching our daughters in the water, I was miles away. When they got out and ran across the lawn into the house, dropping their towels on the grass, and tracking water through the kitchen, I worried about brown spots in the lawn and watermarks on the hardwood, and heard my voice trailing after them, demanding they come back and clean up "right now."

As I attempted to maintain order, David did a lot of running. He'd found a training group in Seattle and was on track to participate in the Portland marathon in October. But then, one morning on a twenty-one-mile practice run, his foot began to hurt. Later, we found out he had a cracked bone and couldn't walk without pain. He was incredibly disappointed. After all the training and anticipation, there was no way he could run. There was nothing either of us could do.

Over the course of the summer, as we continued to grieve for Max, and David slowly let go of his marathon, we found happy moments. When my parents visited, we spent time by the pool. A week later, when Donna, Matt, and their children arrived in a whirlwind, pounding through the kitchen, jumping into the pool, and leaving a trail of clothing behind them, I didn't rush around picking up. David didn't go out for a run either. We both spent time with our friends. Lynn and Adam visited with their children next, followed by another family from UCDS. And with so many people sharing time with our family, we felt supported and connected. But it would take years for the pain to soften and for us to accept we would never have a son or be a family of five.

Contemplation & Conversation

- Has there been a time when you would have given all your money in exchange for a different outcome?

- How has money improved your life? Where has it failed to do so?

Chapter Sixteen

HOME

In 2004, David and I moved to Barcelona with the girls, thrilled to be having an adventure as a family. There was nothing we were avoiding or trying to leave behind and nothing specific we were setting out to find or achieve. Our move was our way of seizing the freedom and advantages of wealth and experiencing the wider, wilder world.

It wasn't hard to bid farewell to Donna and Matt, Lynn and Adam, or my parents: they all had plans to visit. Harder was saying good-bye to our pediatrician, to the guy who had cut my hair for over a decade, and to my therapist. Even more difficult was leaving UCDS. The school had become our family's third place, where we had good friends and the future looked bright. Emily and Ali were set up to go to the right middle school, the right high school, the right college—and with those thoughts, I was thankful to step off the known path.

In the middle of August, I woke up in Barcelona and wandered through the empty living room of our rented seventh-floor apartment looking for David and wondering if the girls were awake. Stepping outside onto the sun-filled terrace, I was clearly in a foreign land. An exotic jumble of leafy plants and palm trees spread out before me and the sounds of a fountain bubbled up from below. On the other side of the park and to the right were rows of apartment buildings, each one connected to the next, most with balconies and yellow awnings, the rooftops an uneven mismatch of chimneys and antenna. Suddenly, a high-pitched squawk sounded through the air. A flock of bright green parrots shot across the sky, skimming the treetops.

"Good morning," David said, stepping outside and giving me a kiss.

"Did you see those green parrots?" I asked.

He'd been up for a couple of hours and was going through boxes, finding plugs and extension cords. Packing in Seattle, we hadn't been sure what to bring and our insecurities were being revealed. David's anxiety was showing up as wires and adaptors. Extension cords were tangled in the girls' toys. Two-, three-, and four-pronged plugs were sprinkled through the kitchen utensils. Meanwhile, my worries had resulted in several boxes of Fiber One cereal hidden in the sheets and towels. Since a weekend getaway could cause irregularity, I wanted to be prepared for an international move.

The parrots and park were highlights, but the apartment was incredible as well. For the first few weeks, in addition to getting lost in the city, we got lost at home. The books we brought filled one shelf in the library, leaving thirty-four others empty. Our clothes looked lonely in their walk-in closets. And with the girls choosing to share a room as they'd always done in Seattle, we had a whole suite ready and waiting for guests—the reason we were renting such a large apartment in the first place.

To fill the void between what we'd brought and all the space we had, we spent a day at IKEA buying red swivel chairs, beds for Emily and Ali, a kitchen table, standing lamps, and desks. Then, searching for a sofa and living room rug at another furniture store, we laughed through several awkward exchanges in Spanish, grappling with the fact that no one was around in August to make deliveries. Later, watching another family arrive, hire a decorator, and instantly furnish a showplace home with sleek sofas, tables, and lamps, I paused. But, in the end, I didn't worry about not doing rich right. We'd had fun buying furniture in a foreign language, doing things our way, together as a family.

Although the girls had been reluctant to leave UCDS, after the first day at the Benjamin Franklin International School, known as BFIS, Ali told us she thought kindergarten was cool. It took Emily longer to adjust, but she eventually bonded with her second-grade teacher. And the community of parents was wonderful. A third of the families were from Spain, a third from the US, and a third from other countries, bringing together an eclectic mix from all over the world. Most who weren't from Spain had been transferred to Barcelona through work, some having lived an expatriate life for years. A few were on sabbatical, taking time away from teaching. A couple were abroad simply for the experience.

"What about you?" a woman asked. "Are you working or is your husband?"

"Actually, neither of us is working. We're here to experience Spain."

"Will you be here a year?"

"We thought so," I said. "But I'm already hoping to stay two." "Wow. A two-year sabbatical. Sounds nice. I'm jealous. How can you manage that?"

Years earlier, I would have found a way to avoid her question, uncomfortable with the facts, afraid of eliciting jealousy or disdain. But standing in the school courtyard under the Spanish sun, believing judgment, guilt, and insecurity were years in the past and an ocean away, I explained we'd moved to Barcelona out of curiosity, excited about having an adventure.

"You must be rich," she said.

I stared at her, feeling that awkward moment.

"We're lucky," I said with a laugh.

"Yes, you are," she said.

For the first few months, while our girls were in school, David and I spent our days exploring the city, wandering through the historic district and visiting museums. We took care of business too, setting up bank accounts, researching how to get Spanish driver's licenses, and figuring out car insurance. As we settled further into the year, David joined the Board at BFIS and became president practically the same day. Soon, he was working Amazon-style hours, helping to improve academics, and hiring a new director. He also studied Spanish and took up flamenco guitar.

Spanish lessons and time at the girls' school were part of my routine as well. Hoping to get to know other parents, I'd raised my hand to help organize the school's Thanksgiving dinner and was shocked when I was asked to chair the event. I didn't yet understand the task was one nobody else wanted or that volunteering wasn't valued in Spain. But by chairing the dinner, I ended up meeting a lot of parents and was proud when the evening turned into a success. I also discovered an art studio near our apartment and spent Thursday mornings creating collages from photographs, my favorite being of Emily and Ali hula hooping on our terrace, the view of the park in the background.

Much of the local culture centered on family and revolved around food. Every Sunday, families came together and spent hours at the table. During the workweek, the midday meal was pivotal as well. People stopped and took time. Stores closed. Restaurants served a menu of the day that included starters, mains, and dessert, making it impossible to rush. And there was no reason to hurry. Nothing was going on from two o'clock until four thirty.

At first, sitting around in the middle of the day didn't feel right. It was uncomfortable not being productive. But, relaxing into the experience, I began to enjoy the slower pace. Long lunches helped build friendships. After a few months, David and I found ourselves lingering over the table with other couples for so long that we often had to scramble to get to BFIS in time to pick up our kids.

Early on, to meet a pediatrician, I asked David to call for an appointment.

"They could get us in next week," he said, setting down the phone with a strange look.

"What's wrong? Don't you think it's important to meet the doctor?"

"It's not that," he said. "They told me we could come in at eight thirty 'in the afternoon,' and we're supposed to bring the girls."

"Eight thirty? At night?"

The doctor's appointment was only the beginning. To help Emily and Ali learn to speak Spanish while doing activities they enjoyed, we signed Ali up for an art class and found horseback riding lessons for Emily. But with days lasting well into what I'd long considered night, and with the Spanish sleeping fewer hours than others in Europe, I was a wreck. Six-year-old Ali's class started at five thirty and didn't end until seven, and riding lessons finished equally late. There was no way to get home, make dinner, eat, read stories, and have the girls tucked into bed by their eight o'clock bedtime. For weeks, trying to be a responsible mother, I sped along the sidewalk, resenting Barcelona afternoons, the girls trailing behind me. How could other parents be sauntering along with their kids, smiling and enjoying the warm evening? How would their kids grow up to be healthy, wealthy, and wise? How was I going to earn my perfect-mother award?

Over time, aware of being stuck in the past, back in Seattle, in a small corner of the world, I let go of the "right" bedtime. Embracing the beauty of long Barcelona afternoons, we took our time getting home. We enjoyed dinner, the bedtime routine, and stories at a more relaxed pace, all of us benefiting from letting go of old habits and beliefs. The girls seemed to get enough sleep too.

Meanwhile, for David and me, late Spanish nights were nothing but fun. Date night in Seattle often meant stopping at the grocery store after dinner to buy milk, stalling to ensure the girls were asleep before we returned home. In Barcelona, where restaurants didn't open until nine o'clock and didn't fill up until eleven, dinner lasted well past the time Emily and Ali were sleeping—and we felt a lot younger, sexier, and better-connected as we strolled through the city at midnight.

Spanish mornings were a welcome change too. I'd never been early to rise, and in Spain, there was no rush to get up and get going. Even Starbucks didn't open until eight in the morning. And with no value placed on the efficiency of drinking coffee on the run, I began to understand that what I'd considered human nature was American culture. Living in a country where customs and norms were unfamiliar, it was obvious there was no "right" way of getting things done—no one happy life.

As we grew accustomed to unfamiliar routines, we shared the experience with other BFIS parents, all of us trying to learn the language and adapt to the culture. Without the same need to adhere to old rules, without the same expectations and preconceptions, we quickly felt part of our new community. That year, I didn't send Christmas cards—and was beginning to feel more carefree.

Happy with the rhythm of long lunches and late nights and getting to know other families, the decision to stay in Barcelona a second year was easy. Then, after that second year, feeling part of the BFIS community and connected as a family of four, we stayed a third and fourth year as well. At the end of the school year in 2008, with Emily about to start middle school, David finishing his work as president of the board at BFIS, and me interested in taking writing classes in English, we planned our return to the United States. But a window was open. No longer tied to a traditional path, we took further advantage of our freedom. Rather than move back to Seattle, we spent a year traveling around the world, "roadschooling" Emily and Ali, doing volunteer work as a family, and spending months at a time in several different countries.

A sixty-day visa allowed us to spend two months in China teaching at a kindergarten in Xi'an for two weeks then renting an apartment in Shanghai for six. From there, we visited Vietnam, where we had donated money to build a house for a family and spent a day painting the trim and meeting the new homeowners. For two months, we lived in Sydney, where David's mom and my parents joined us for Thanksgiving. We spent Christmas in Tahiti with Lynn, Adam, and their kids. From there, it was New Zealand, where we lived on four separate sheep farms, staying in people's homes. We met up with good friends from BFIS in Bali, traveled through Mumbai and Jordan, and returned to Barcelona for two months before heading to South America to visit my brother who was working in the foreign service in Bolivia. Then, nostalgic for long Spanish lunches and late Spanish nights, missing our friends and community at BFIS, we return to Barcelona for one more year.

During our travels, we'd read books on Kindles, and when we visited an orphanage in Guayaquil, Ecuador, and learned the library was locked and none of the girls had access to books, David starting thinking. In the fall of 2009, he and Colin, another BFIS parent, came up with the idea of using technology to get books into the hands of children in the developing world. They created a pilot program at BFIS and launched another at a school in Accra, Ghana. Over the months that followed, Colin left his job as director of ESADE business school to work full-time on the project and the two of them began building a team, visiting schools in Ghana, and meeting with the Ghanaian government.

In the spring of 2011, when Emily and Ali returned to our Barcelona apartment at eight o'clock after horseback riding lessons and soccer practice, David was still at work. He'd found his next Big Thing, championing digital reading in underserved communities.

Wealth had shaped our life, adding ease and opportunity, compelling me to get clear about myself and my values. I had confirmed where happiness existed—within relationships, community, and a sense of purpose. It didn't matter where we were in the world. As I closed my computer, hugged the girls, and began to make dinner, I felt at home. I too had found my next Big Thing, excited to be writing, hoping to share my story.

Contemplation & Conversation

- Does the way you spend money match your values?

- What would you do if you had all the money in the world?

WHAT'S NEXT?

In the summer of 2011, we returned to the United States. That fall, as the girls settled into school, the Occupy Wall Street movement began in Zuccotti Park in New York City, protesting corporate greed and inequality. Now, with Trump in the White House, social and economic inequality has become an even more acute problem. An unprecedented amount of money has been amassed at the top, the rich controlling as much wealth as they did before the Great Depression.

I'm not an economist or a politician, but given all this wealth, no one in our country should be going hungry or be without healthcare. Everyone deserves access to housing and a good education. I support the idea of wealth redistribution and believe the rich need to pay higher taxes. It even sounds reasonable to say billionaires shouldn't exist. But we need to let go of the anger and resentment that divides us.

The phrase "the one percent" has become divisive, fostering a sense of "us" versus "them," blaming one socioeconomic group for problems created over years by a system that is no longer working. Talking about "them" only further solidifies deeply rooted stereotypes.

When we don't have personal connections to anyone with money, and the only rich we see are the glamorous and glitzy in movies and the corrupt in the news, it's natural, even validating, to presume the worst. The Kardashians appear so typical of the rich—self-centered, materialistic, and always out for more. The Sackler family of Purdue Pharma selling OxyContin, and the wealthy parents who used money to fake test scores and bribe coaches to get their unqualified children into prestigious colleges also confirm the link we have come to expect between wealth and dishonesty.

Studies show people in lower-income groups view the rich with envy and distrust. When asked to evaluate different companies and industries, most linked profit to social harm, evil, and wrongdoing. Anecdotally, I feel the judgment too. A friend just told me a man boarding a flight in front of her muttered "F*ck you" to those he was passing in first class. No one confronted him for being rude or inappropriate. In fact, someone laughed. When I recently asked another friend about a tennis opponent, she said, "She's rich," and went on to complain about her obnoxious, superior attitude on the court.

"All she does is play tennis and take lessons," my friend added.

Perhaps this woman's financial situation allowed her to take lessons, but was money the cause of her obnoxious behavior?

With the ability to pay for the services and support that most people rely on from friends and neighbors, people with money have blind spots. We can be insular and out of touch, which I don't say with pride. We tend to be isolated too, which I don't say with pleasure. But in reading research on how the wealthy lack empathy and have questionable morals, I am aware of unconscious biases.

In a 2012 UC Berkeley study examining the influence of money on our thinking and behavior, psychologist Paul Piff had two strangers play a game of Monopoly. One was randomly selected to be the rich player. This rich player was given twice as much money at the start of the game, could collect twice the salary when passing GO, and had two dice to roll instead of one. As the game progressed and he was winning, the rich player became increasingly boisterous, even rude to the other player. Not only was his attitude self-centered and entitled, his understanding of the situation was warped. The game had clearly been rigged in his favor, and yet he believed he had earned his success—all of which sounds so typical of the rich. But could the feeling of winning have been a factor? Anyone can get excited about a victory and exhibit poor sportsmanship, especially when competition and success are so highly valued.

As for empathy, everyone is influenced by their cultural context and personal relationships. It makes sense that those facing hardship are more empathetic to suffering than those who have no connection to need. Research has found that when exposed to adversity, the wealthy become more empathetic. What's more, those living in socioeconomically diverse areas gave more money to charity than their counterparts in homogeneously high-end neighborhoods, and when shown a video on child poverty, the wealthy gave money at a rate equal to lower-income participants.

As we take a hard look at capitalism, democracy, and the kind of society we want to live within, we need to explore money at a personal, individual level. Talking about money is challenging for everyone. Most Americans think it's rude. Many don't even know how much their partner makes. Maybe we are ashamed of how much or how little we have, embarrassed by our over-spending, or fear being judged as not measuring up. There will be awkward moments. But if we were to treat our rent and our salaries as facts to compare and discuss, we could learn from one another. We could build stronger relationships too. A con-versation about money might be one of the most intimate and rewarding to be had, allowing us to let down our guard and truly connect. But if we continue to stay quiet, to keep money in the dark, wrapped in mystery to be glorified or vilified, we allow stereotypes to persist. Our silence perpetuates divides.

Thinking back to before we met with other couples to talk about giving money to our kids, to before I had the courage to tell my brother how I felt about his reaction to our gifts, and to when there was more silence around money between me and my parents, I remember wondering why Lynn and Adam, Donna and Matt, and David and I were so quiet about our wealth. Our situations were similar. We were good friends. Why exactly weren't we speaking more candidly about the huge change that had occurred in our lives? Were we trying to avoid potential rivalry and competition, hoping to keep judg-ment and jealousy outside of our relationships? Was it helpful to allow mystery to remain? Shouldn't friendship mean more than our relative financial standing? Wouldn't we have been better off treating money as a tool and sharing our financial questions and doubts? By talking, maybe we could have put money in its place and connected with one another in a more intimate way. Maybe that intimacy scared us. As it was, for decades, we stayed quiet, not benefitting from one another's perspectives, keeping the specifics unknown, and giving wealth more power than we were giving ourselves or each other.

By sharing our stories, breaking the taboo, and talking about money, we could find new ways to connect and start closing divides. F. Scott Fitzgerald got it wrong when he said, "Let me tell you about the very rich. They are different from you and me." Yes, the rich have more money, but we all have the same needs, fears, and dreams. In our desire for acceptance and love, for being part of a community, and for meaning and purpose in our lives, we are all ninety-nine percent the same.

ACKNOWLEDGMENTS

For the last decade, writing has been my challenge and joy, and I'm thankful for all who have been part of the journey—especially those who have shared their stories with me.

I want to give a special thanks to Rachel Greenwald for helping me get started, to Shawn Chereskin, Dianna O'Doherty, and Stephanie Beaurain for being early readers, and to my parents and very dear friend Maurien Møller and her husband Boris for their unwavering support. Thank you, Jay Schaefer, for your wisdom and encouragement. Your dedication kept me going. Thank you also to Lewis Buzbee, Patricia Mickelberry, and Marion Roach Smith for your editing help.

My deepest gratitude goes to my agent, Sorche Fairbank, whose insight, guidance, and belief in me and my story made all the difference, to my publisher, Red Hen Press, and editor, Kate Gale, for being smart, fearless champions, and to my husband and daughters for their acceptance and love. You are my everything.

BIOGRAPHICAL NOTE

PHOTO BY KELLY VORVES

Jennifer Risher was born in Seattle, Washington, grew up in Oregon, and graduated from Connecticut College. She joined Microsoft in 1991 where she worked as a recruiter and then as a product manager. She and her husband, David, have two daughters and live in San Francisco, where David is CEO of Worldreader, a nonprofit he cofounded with a mission to create a world where everyone is a reader. *We Need to Talk* is Jennifer's first book.